# BOOKS BY JOACHIM JEREMIAS

*Rediscovering the Parables*

*The Eucharistic Words of Jesus*

*The Central Message of the New Testament*

*The Parables of Jesus*

# REDISCOVERING THE PARABLES

JOACHIM JEREMIAS

Charles Scribner's Sons · NEW YORK

3 5 7 9 11 13 15 17 19  M/P  20 18 16 14 12 10 8 6 4

*Printed in the United States of America*
ISBN 0-684-15129-4

*Library of Congress Catalog Card Number: 67-13197*

# CONTENTS

## I THE PROBLEM

## II THE RETURN TO JESUS FROM THE PRIMITIVE CHURCH

1 The Translation of the Parables into Greek    17
2 Representational Changes    18
3 Embellishment    19
4 Influence of the Old Testament and of Folk-story Themes    22
5 The Change of Audience    24
6 The Hortatory Use of the Parables by the Church    32
7 The Influence of the Church's Situation    36
   A The Delay in Christ's Return    36
   B The Missionary Church    50
   C Regulations for the Leadership of the Church    53
8 Allegorizing    54
9 Collection and Fusion of Parables    71
   A Double Parables    71
   B Collections of Parables    73
   C Fusion of Parables    74
10 The Setting    76
   A Secondary Context    77
   B Secondary Situations and Transitions    78
   C Introductory Formulae    79
   D The Conclusion of the Parables    80

**6** *Contents*

## III THE MESSAGE OF THE PARABLES OF JESUS

| | | |
|---|---|---|
| 1 | Now Is the Day of Salvation | 89 |
| 2 | God's Mercy for Sinners | 97 |
| 3 | The Great Assurance | 116 |
| 4 | In Sight of Disaster | 127 |
| 5 | It May Be Too Late | 135 |
| 6 | The Challenge of the Hour | 142 |
| 7 | Realized Discipleship | 156 |
| 8 | The Via Dolorosa and Exaltation of the Son of Man | 172 |
| 9 | The Consummation | 173 |
| 10 | Parabolic Actions | 179 |

## IV CONCLUSION

*Appendices*

| | | |
|---|---|---|
| A | Glossary | 185 |
| B | Index of Synoptic Parables | 189 |

# PREFACE

THE WISH has often been expressed that *The Parables of Jesus* should be made available to a wider circle of readers, especially to those who do not know Greek. This edition, which is designed to meet that wish, has been abridged by the omission of the book's purely technical and linguistic content. The revision was undertaken by my assistant Dr Berndt Schaller, in co-operation with me. The corresponding adaptation of Professor S. H. Hooke's translation of the original book (revised edition, 1963) is by Mr Frank Clarke. He has also offered numerous suggestions to make the book more readable for which I am particularly grateful.

My aim has been to go back to the oldest form of the parables attainable and to try to recover what Jesus himself meant by them. With this in view, I have laid special emphasis on interpreting them against their local Palestinian background. The outcome of this is presented in Part III, which the reader is strongly advised to read immediately after the introductory Part I. When he then goes on to the critical analysis in Part II, he will realize, I hope, that the aim of this, too, is simply to provide as reliable an approach as possible to Jesus' own words. Only the Son of man himself and his word can give authority to our preaching.

JOACHIM JEREMIAS

# I

## THE PROBLEM

THE student of the parables of Jesus, as they have been transmitted to us in the first three Gospels, is standing on a particularly firm historical foundation. The parables are part of the bed-rock of tradition. This is no surprise; it is a fact that pictures leave a deeper impress on the mind than abstractions. In the case of Jesus' parables in particular, it must be added that they throughout reflect with peculiar clarity the character of his good news, the eschatological nature of his preaching, the intensity of his call to repentance, and his conflict with Pharisaism. Everywhere behind the Greek text we get glimpses of the Aramaic that was Jesus' mother-tongue. Besides this, the parables' imagery is drawn from the daily life of Palestine. Take the sower in Mark 4.3-8, for example. Curiously enough, he sows so clumsily that much of the seed is wasted; we might have expected a description of the regular method of sowing, and that, in fact, is what we have here. This is easily understood when we realize that in Palestine sowing precedes ploughing. So, in the parable, the sower strides over the unploughed stubble, and with this in mind we can comprehend why 'some seed fell along the path'; he sows intentionally on the path that the villagers have trodden over the stubble, since he intends to plough up the path with the rest of the field. He sows intentionally among the thorns standing withered in the fallow, because they too will be ploughed up. Nor need it surprise us that some grain falls on rocky ground; the underlying limestone, thinly covered with soil, hardly shows above the surface till the ploughshare jars against it. What seems to the western mind to be bad farming is simply customary usage in Palestinian conditions.

Further, Jesus' parables are something entirely new. In all the rabbinic literature, not one single parable has come down to us from the period before Jesus; only two similes from Rabbi Hillel (*c.* 20 BC), who jokingly compared the body with a statue, and the soul with a guest. It is among the sayings of Rabban Jochanan ben Zakkai (d.*c.* AD 80) that we first meet with a parable (see p. 149 below). As its imagery resembles one of Jesus' parables, we may well ask whether Jesus' model (together with other factors, such as Greek animal fables) did not have an important influence on the rabbi's adopting parables as a narrative form.

The uniqueness of Jesus' parables comes out clearly when they are compared with analogous productions from the same period and cultural context, such as the Pauline similitudes or the rabbinic parables. Comparison reveals a definite personal style, a singular clarity and simplicity, a matchless mastery of construction. The conclusion is inevitable that we are dealing with particularly trustworthy tradition. We are standing right before Jesus when reading his parables.

Not only do the parables of Jesus, regarded as a whole, represent a specially reliable tradition, but they also appear to be entirely free from problematic aspects. The hearers find themselves in a familiar scene where everything is so clear and simple that a child can understand it, and so obvious that again and again those who hear cannot help saying 'Yes, that's how it is'. Yet the parables confront us with a difficult problem, namely, the recovery of their original meaning.

Even in the very earliest period, during the first decades after the death of Jesus, the parables underwent a certain amount of reinterpretation. At a very early stage the process had begun of treating them as allegories—of attributing some special significance to every detail (for an example see pp. 24f. below); and for centuries that kind of allegorical interpretation obscured their real meaning like a thick veil.

Many circumstances contributed to this. At first there may
have been an unconscious wish to discover a deeper meaning
in the simple words of Jesus. In the Hellenistic world it was
usual to interpret myths as vehicles of secret knowledge, and
in Hellenistic Judaism allegorical exegesis was highly
esteemed; hence people expected that Christian teachers
would resort to the same method. In the succeeding period a
stimulus was given to this tendency by the fact that there
were four Gospel parables which were accompanied by a
detailed allegorical interpretation of their individual
features (Mark 4.14–20 par.; Matt. 13.37–43, 49–50;
John 10.7–18). But above all, it was the 'hardening' theory
(Mark 4.10–12 par.; cf. v. 34) which led to the predominance
of the allegorical method of interpretation.

In its present context, Mark 4.11b-12 purports to say
that Jesus spoke in parables in order to conceal the mystery
of the Kingdom of God from 'those outside' and to harden
their hearts. That is to say that Jesus' parables had a hidden
meaning that could be discovered only with the help of
allegorical interpretation. But it can be shown, and in fact
scholars all but universally recognize this, that Mark 4.11b-
12 originally was an independent saying, and that it was
Mark who inscrted it into ch. 4 with the parables. This
happened through the Greek word *parabolē* (parable),
which corresponds to the Aramaic word *mathla*, which, as
we shall see (pp. 13f.), has a variety of connotations and can
mean both 'parable' and 'riddle'. In our passage it originally
meant 'riddle'. If, then, we proceed from the Aramaic,[1]
Mark 4.11b-12 means 'God has given to you the secret of his
Kingdom, but to those who are outside, everything is puzzling,
so that (as it is written) "they see but do not perceive, and hear
but do not understand, unless they turn around and God[2]

[1] On the linguistic evidence for the translation, see *The Parables of
Jesus*, London and New York, 1963, pp. 14ff.

[2] The full significance of many of Jesus' sayings can be realized only
when we remember that he very often uses the passive in reverential
turns of speech when God's actions are in question. We have an
example here in the passive construction 'and be forgiven'.

forgives them" '. If it is understood like this, the saying refers to the whole of Jesus' preaching, and means
that his proclamation of God's rule that is even now
beginning can be understood only by believers, and is
bound to remain a riddle to unbelievers. If this interpretation is correct, the words reported in Mark 4. 11b-12 were
not originally spoken with reference to the parables, and
therefore do not justify us in looking behind them for a
hidden secret meaning to be grasped only by means of an
allegorical exposition.

It is to Adolf Jülicher that we owe the final discarding of
the allegorical method of interpretation. It is positively dis-
tressing to read in his chapter on the 'History of the Interpretation of the Parables of Jesus'[1] the story of the centuries of
distortion and ill-usage which the parables have suffered
through this method. Only against such a background is it
possible to estimate the extent of the liberation achieved
when Jülicher not only proved incontestably by hundreds of
cases that allegorizing leads to error, but also maintained
the fundamental position that it is utterly alien to the
parables of Jesus. Although the emphasis may have been
one-sided, his work remains fundamental; isolated reversions
to the allegorical method in recent studies only serve to
confirm this judgment.

But, as none has shown better than C. H. Dodd, Jülicher
left the work half done. His efforts to free the parables from
the fantastic and arbitrary interpretations of every detail
caused him to fall into a fatal error. In his view, the surest
safeguard against such arbitrary treatment lies in regarding
the parables as a piece of real life and in drawing from each
of them a single idea; this idea must be of the widest possible
generality (here lies the error): the broadest application will
prove to be the true one. 'The story of the Rich Man and
Poor Lazarus was intended to induce joy in a life of suffering,
fear of the life of pleasure' (Luke 16.19–31). That 'even the

---

[1] A. Jülicher, *Die Gleichnisreden Jesu* I, Tübingen, 1899 (= 1910,
1963), pp. 203–322.

richest of men is at every moment wholly dependent on the power and mercy of God' is the lesson of the parable of the Rich Fool (Luke 12.16ff.). 'Wise use of the present as the condition of a happy future' is the lesson of the parable of the Unjust Steward (Luke 16.1-8). The original form of Matt. 24.45-51 was intended to stir up the disciples to 'the most earnest fulfilment of their duty toward God'. 'A reward is only earned by performance' is the fundamental idea of the parable of the Talents (Matt. 25.14ff.). We are told that the parables announce a genuine religious humanity; they are stripped of their eschatological import. Jesus is imperceptibly transformed into an 'apostle of progress' (Jülicher), a teacher of wisdom who inculcates moral precepts and a simplified theology by means of striking metaphors and stories. But nothing could be less like him. Unfortunately, Jülicher stopped half way; he rid the parables of the thick layer of dust with which the allegorical interpretation had covered them, but after accomplishing that preliminary task he did not go forward. The main task is still before us: we must try to recover the parables' original meaning. How can this be done?

Jülicher's work was so outstanding that for a long time no important special studies of the parables appeared. At last the form-criticism school essayed an advance by classifying them into categories. A distinction was drawn between simile, comparison, parable, similitude, allegory, illustration, and so on—a fruitless labour in the end, since the Hebrew *mashal* (Aramaic *mathla*) embraced all these categories and many more without distinction. The word may mean in the ordinary language of post-biblical Judaism, without resorting to a formal classification, figurative forms of speech of every kind: parable, comparison, allegory, fable, proverb, apocalyptic revelation, riddle, pseudonym, symbol, fictitious person, example, theme, argument, apology, refutation, jest. Similarly the Greek *parabolē* in the New Testament has not only the meaning 'parable', but also 'comparison' (Luke 5.36; Mark 3.23) and 'symbol' (Heb.

9.9; 11.19; cf. Mark 13.28); in Luke 4.23 it should be rendered 'proverb' or 'commonplace', in 6.39 'proverb'; in Mark 7.17 it means 'riddle', and in Luke 14.7 simply 'rule'. (I must expressly emphasize that in this study the word 'parable' is used in the broader sense of *mashal/mathla*.) To force the parables of Jesus into the categories of Greek rhetoric is to impose on them an alien law. Indeed, no progress was achieved along this line. The important fundamental insights that we owe to the form-criticism school have not so far been fruitfully applied to the study of the parables.

The point of view that decisively opened the way to further advance was, if I am not mistaken, first put forward by A. T. Cadoux,[1] who laid down the principle that the parables must be placed in the setting of Jesus' life. Unfortunately, the way in which Cadoux attempted to develop this correct perception in his book was open to objections, so that the value of his work was limited to acute comments on details. B. T. D. Smith followed more cautiously along this line,[2] and in many passages succeeded in illuminating the historical background of the parables; it is the more to be regretted that he confined himself to their imagery, and did not deal with their theological interpretation. But it was C. H. Dodd's book, *The Parables of the Kingdom*,[3] which achieved a break-through in the direction first indicated by Cadoux. In this extraordinarily significant book a really successful attempt was made for the first time to put the parables into the setting of Jesus' life; and this introduced a new era in their interpretation. Dodd, however, confined his attention to the parables of the Kingdom of Heaven; and the one-sided nature of his conception of the Kingdom (all the emphasis being laid on the view that in the works of Jesus the Kingdom had now finally been ushered in) resulted in a foreshortening of his whole view, and this has continued to influence his otherwise masterly interpretation.

[1] *The Parables of Jesus. Their Art and Use*, New York, 1931.
[2] *The Parables of the Synoptic Gospels*, Cambridge, 1937.
[3] London, 1935.

What we have to deal with is a conception which is essentially simple but has far-reaching consequences. It is that the parables of Jesus are not—at any rate primarily—literary productions, and that it is not their object to lay down general maxims; but that each of them was uttered in an actual situation in Jesus' life, at a particular and often unforeseen point. Moreover, as we shall see, they were mostly concerned with a situation of conflict—with justification, defence, attack, and even challenge. For the most part, though not exclusively, they are weapons of controversy. Every one of them calls for an answer on the spot.

The recognition of this fact is the starting point for what we have to do. Jesus spoke to men of flesh and blood; he addressed himself to the situation of the moment. Each of his parables has a definite historical setting, and to recover that setting is the task before us.[1] What did Jesus intend to say at this or that particular moment? What effect must his words have had on his hearers? These are the questions that we must ask, so that we may, as far as possible, recover the original meaning of the parables, and hear again his authentic voice.

[1] It is perhaps possible by glancing at the collection of parables in Matt. 13 to explain the problem thus: it is as though all that remained to us of the preaching of a celebrated preacher of our time were a collection of illustrative stories. Such a collection could give us an idea of their full value only if we knew in every case what ideas of the preacher were intended to be illustrated by each individual example. In the same way we shall not understand each individual parable in the collection of Matt. 13 aright unless we can reconstruct for ourselves the situation in which Jesus uttered it.

# II

## THE RETURN TO JESUS
## FROM THE PRIMITIVE CHURCH

As THEY have come down to us, Jesus' parables have a double historical setting. (1) The original historical setting of the parables, as of all his utterances, is some specific situation in the course of his activity. Many of the parables are so vividly told that it is natural to assume that they arise out of some actual occurrence.[1] (2) But subsequently, before they assumed a written form, they 'lived' in the primitive Church, which proclaimed, preached, and taught the words of Jesus in its missionary activities, its assemblies, and in its catechetical instruction. It collected and arranged his sayings under specific headings, and created settings for them, sometimes modifying their form, expanding here, allegorizing there, always in relation to its own situation between the cross and the second coming of Christ. In our study of the parables it is important to bear in mind the difference between the situation of Jesus and that of the primitive Church. In not a few cases it will be necessary to remove his sayings and parables from their setting in the life and thought of the primitive Church, and try to recover their original setting in the life of Jesus, if we are to hear once more his original tones and experience anew the vital qualities of force, conflict, and authority in the historical events. As soon as we try to ascertain the original historical setting of the

---

[1] The Unjust Steward (Luke 16. 1ff., cf. pp. 143ff.), the Tares among the Wheat (Matt. 13.24ff., cf. pp. 176ff.), the Burglar (Matt. 24.43f., cf. p. 37); perhaps, too, the Rich Fool (Luke 12.16ff.) and the Good Samaritan (Luke 10.30f.).

parables, we meet with certain definite principles of transformation.

A great help in this connection is that the Gospel of
Thomas[1] provides us with an independent tradition for the
following eleven synoptic parables:

Passage  9  (8) The Sower (cf. p. 20).
         20 (20) The Mustard Seed (cf. p. 116).
         21b and 103 (22 and 100) The Burglar (cf. pp. 69, 75).
         57 (58) The Tares among the Wheat (cf. p. 176).
         63 (64) The Rich Fool (cf. p. 129 n.3).
         64 (65) The Great Supper (cf. pp. 138ff).
         65 (66) The Wicked Husbandmen (cf. pp. 57f.).
         76 (76) The Pearl (cf. p. 156f.).
         96 (93) The Leaven (cf. p. 116).
      107 (104) The Lost Sheep (cf. p. 105).
      109 (106) The Treasure (cf. p. 23).

|  | Synoptic | Gospel of Thomas |
|---|---|---|
| Mark[2] | 6 | 3 |
| Material common to Matt.-Luke | 9 | 4 |
| Special Matt. | 10 | 3 |
| Special Luke | 14 | 1 |

## 1 The Translation of the Parables into Greek

Jesus spoke Galilean Aramaic. The task of translating his
sayings into Greek, which began at an early date, necessarily
involved, sometimes to a considerable but generally only to

---

[1] The first number of each passage is that given in *The Gospel
according to Thomas*, Coptic Text edited and translated by A. Guil-
laumont, H.-Ch. Puech, G. Quispel, W. Till and †Yassah 'Abd al
Masih, Leiden, 1959. The one following in brackets is that of J.
Leipoldt, used by R. M. Grant and D. N. Freedman, *The Secret
Sayings of Jesus according to the Gospel of Thomas*, London, 1960.
[2] Partly taken over by Matthew and Luke; see the list of synoptic
parables at the end of the book (p. 185).

a slight degree, innumerable changes of meaning. Hence the
retranslation of the parables into Jesus' mother-tongue is
an important, perhaps the most important, aid to the
recovery of their original meaning.

Although every intelligent person will realize the tentative
nature of such retranslations, it cannot be denied that they rest
on a firm foundation. In particular, the numerous variations in
translation which occur in the gospel tradition provide reliable
information about the underlying Aramaic wording. Unfortunately this important aid is not yet adequately appreciated, still
less systematically used.[1]


## 2  *Representational Changes*

It was inevitable that in the process of translation into
Greek, not only the vocabulary of Jesus' sayings, but also
the Palestinian background embodied in them should be
'translated' into terms of the Hellenistic environment. Thus
in the Lukan parables we find turns of phrase that presuppose
Hellenistic building technique,[2] Roman law-court procedure,[3] and non-Palestinian horticulture[4] and landscapes.[5]
In Mark we meet with the Roman division of the night into
four watches (Mark 13.35; cf. 6.48), based on the require-

---

[1] In the present edition, the linguistic material can be quoted only
occasionally; it is treated in detail in the complete edition.

[2] Luke 6.47f.; 11.33: houses with cellars (not usual in Palestine);
8.16; 11.33: a house with an entrance passage from which the light
shines out on people coming in.

[3] Luke 12.58: 'bailiff' (otherwise in Matt. 5.25: 'guard' = 'synagogue
official').

[4] Luke 13.19: in Luke a man sows a mustard-seed 'in his garden';
this agrees with the fact that in the Hellenistic world mustard is included
among the garden-herbs. In Palestine, on the other hand, the cultivation
of mustard in garden-beds was forbidden. Luke 14.35: there is no
Palestinian evidence for the use of salt as manure.

[5] Luke 6.48: the river overflowing its bank (otherwise in Matt. 7.25:
'cloud-burst').

ments of Roman military service (cf. Acts 12.4), instead of
the Palestinian[1] division into three (Luke 12.38)—one of the
numerous indications that the second Gospel was not
written in Palestine. In such cases we shall prefer the
Palestinian description of the situation.

But here we must go cautiously. We shall see, for instance,
that Jesus repeatedly and intentionally uses by way of
illustration Levantine methods of punishment, regarded by
the Jews as particularly cruel (see pp. 142, 165f.). Non-
Palestinian conditions, therefore, do not always indicate
editorial revision or lack of authenticity. We can reach a
fairly reliable judgment only in those cases where the
tradition is divided.

## 3 Embellishment

In the parable of the servants to whom money was entrusted,
the Matthean version tells of three servants, of whom the
first received five talents, the second two, and the third one—
that is to say 50,000, 20,000, and 10,000 denarii respectively
(Matt. 25.15); in Luke we have ten servants who receive
only 100 denarii each (Luke 19.13). The continuation of the
story in Luke (19.16–21) shows that the number of servants
(three) in Matthew is original; similarly with regard to the
amounts, the smaller sum (as in Luke) must be original,
since in both versions the amount is expressly stated to
be quite small (Matt. 25.21, 23 par. Luke 19.17); 10,000–
50,000 denarii hardly agrees with this. In Luke, then, the
number of servants has increased, and in Matthew the sums
involved are immensely magnified; the oriental story-
teller's delight in large numbers has thus led to embellishment in both versions of the story. Pleasure in embellishment also played a part in the secondary expansion which
the parable of the Great Supper has undergone in Matthew.

[1] Judg. 7.19; Jub. 49.10, 12.

In Luke (14.16) and in the Gospel of Thomas (64) the host is a private individual, but in Matt. 22.2 he is a king (see p. 139). The change from 'householder' to 'king' must be regarded as the same kind of shift in the tradition as we meet with in rabbinical literature where parables of daily life are changed into parables in which a king figures; it is truly oriental. Finally, in the version of this parable in the Gospel of Thomas the excuses are narrated much more vividly than in Matthew and Luke, and the rural setting becomes an urban one (see below pp. 138ff.). There is another example of embellishment in the parable of the Sower as told in the Gospel of Thomas (9): 'Jesus said, "See, the sower went out; he filled his hand and threw [the seed out]. Some [seeds] fell on the road; the birds came and gathered them. Others fell on the rock and did not strike root in the earth, and sent up no ears to heaven. And others fell on the thorns; they choked the seed, and the worm ate them. And others fell on the good earth, and it brought forth good fruit going up to heaven; it bore sixty per measure and one hundred and twenty per measure." ' Here, in addition to the synoptic writers' version, we have the antithesis ('did not strike root in the earth, and sent up no ears to heaven'), the mention of the worm, and the increase in number, 120. Sometimes the additions are rather trivial; for example, the metaphor about divided service (Matt. 6.24; Luke 16.13) appears in the Gospel of Thomas (47a) as: 'It is impossible for a man to mount two horses [at once], and to stretch two bows [at once], and it is impossible for a servant to serve two masters. . . .'

Among the cases of embellishment, we have to include the use of stylistic expedients that are supposed to enliven the narrative. An example is the insertion of the words 'They said to him' in Matt. 21.41, which are not in Mark 12.9 or Luke 20.16. Through their introduction Jesus' hearers are made to pass judgment on themselves without realizing it—a feature that is found both in the Old Testament (e.g. the prophet Nathan's parable, II Sam. 12.5ff.; the parable of the woman of Tekoa, II Sam. 14.8ff.; the parable

of one of the sons of the prophets, I Kings 20.40) and in
other parables of Jesus (Matt. 21.31; Luke 7.43).

At the same time, our quest calls for great caution. It is,
indeed, a special characteristic of Jesus' use of parables that
they are drawn from life, but show numerous unusual
features, intended to arouse the attention of the hearers and
carrying for the most part special emphasis. It is not an
everyday occurrence that all the guests should brusquely
refuse an invitation (see pp. 140f.), and that the householder (or the king) should call in to his table anyone who
happened to be in the streets (Matt. 22.9; Luke 14.21–23);
that the maidens awaiting the bridegroom should one and
all fall asleep (Matt. 25.5), and the bridegroom should refuse
to admit late-comers to the wedding (Matt. 25.12; cf. Luke
13.25); that a guest should present himself in a filthy garment at the marriage of the king's son (Matt. 22.11ff.); and
that a grain of corn should yield a hundredfold (Mark 4.8;
cf. Gen. 26.12). Such gross exaggerations are still characteristic of the oriental way of telling a story, and their frequent
occurrence in the parables shows that Jesus intentionally
adopted this style. The element of unexpectedness that they
display was intended to indicate where the meaning was to
be found. This appears most forcibly in the parable of the
Wicked Servant. The 'servant' (see p. 164) is said (Matt.
18.23f.) to owe ten thousand talents (=a hundred million
denarii), and the monstrous nature of this fantastic sum
becomes apparent when we remember that in 4 BC Galilee
and Peraea paid no more than two hundred talents a year
in taxes—a fiftieth of that sum! But the vastness of the
amount is intentional. It is meant to impress on the hearers
by 'shock tactics' that man cannot pay his debt to God, and
it throws into strong relief the sharp contrast with the
fellow-servant's trivial debt of a hundred denarii. Thus it by
no means follows that a mass rejection of the uncommon
features in Jesus' parables is called for; on the contrary, such
hints at the interpretation may well be original. However, a
comparison of the parallel forms in which the parables have

come down to us does show that in many cases they have been elaborated, and that the simpler version is probably the original one.

## 4 *Influence of the Old Testament and of Folk-story Themes*

In some of the parables there are references to Scripture (Mark 4.29, 32; 12.1, 9a, 10f. par.; Matt. 25.31, 46, cf. Luke 13.27, 29). The remarkably small number of these passages is reduced by the fact that of the four just named from Matthew and Luke, at least three, if not all four, are secondary. But besides this, seeing that the case is different in the Gospel of Thomas, the other passages, too, need careful examination. For the version of the parable of the Vineyard in the Gospel of Thomas (65), like the Lukan form (20.9), does not give the detailed account, taken from Isa. 5.1f. (Mark 12.1 par. Matt. 21.33), of the construction of the vineyard, nor does it give the closing question based on Isa. 5.5 (Mark 12.9 par.); and the subsequent quotation from Ps. 118.22f. appears as an independent saying (66). Since, as this saying shows, the Gospel of Thomas does not object on principle to quoting Scripture, and especially since in the Synoptic Gospels Isa. 5.1f., 5 and Ps. 118.22f. are quoted, not from the Hebrew, but from the Greek text, these Scripture references hardly belong to the original form of the tradition. As to the parable of the Mustard-seed in the Gospel of Thomas (20), the conclusion reads: '. . . it produces a large branch and becomes a shelter for the birds of heaven.' This is presumably a free allusion to Dan. 4.9, 18; Ezek. 17.23, 31.6; in Mark (4.32) the reference to Ezek. 17.23 and Dan. 4.9, 18 appears more clearly, in Matthew (13.32) and Luke (13.19) it has developed into a free quotation of Dan. 4.18. The inaccurate description of the mustard-plant as a tree—this occurs only in Matthew and

Luke, not in Mark or the Gospel of Thomas—is also derived
from Dan. 4.17. Finally, in the parable of the Leaven, the
immense quantity of three measures (*se'a*) of meal (Matt.
13.33; Luke 13.21) is not mentioned in the Gospel of Thomas
(96); it is likely to come from Gen. 18.6. So we see that there
is a tendency to illustrate by or to add Scripture references.
This does not exclude the possibility that Jesus himself
occasionally referred to Scripture in a parable. Indeed, this
is very probable in at least two cases: at the end of the parable
of the Mustard-seed (see above), and at the end of the parable
of the Seed growing of itself (Mark 4.29 cit. Joel 3.13).

Side by side with such references to Scripture, occasional
*folk-story themes* found their way into the parables. We shall
repeatedly find that Jesus himself made use of such themes;
but in at least two cases they can be shown to be secondary.

The version of the parable of the Treasure as given in the
Gospel of Thomas (109) is utterly degenerated. It tells of a
man who bought a field, and later discovered by chance in
his property a treasure that made him a rich man. This has
hardly anything in common with the Matthean version,
which is certainly original. On the other hand, the new
version corresponds with a story told in a rabbinic commentary on the Song of Solomon:

| *Gospel of Thomas* 109 | *Commentary on Song of Solomon* 4.12 |
|---|---|
| The kingdom is like a man who had a treasure, of which he knew nothing, hidden in his field. And after he died he left it to his son. | It (i.e. the situation described in S. of S. 4.12) is like a man who inherited a place full of rubbish. |
| The son (also) knew nothing (about it). He took that field and sold it. | The inheritor was lazy and sold it for a ridiculously small sum. |
| And the buyer went to plough and found the treasure. | The buyer dug it industriously and found a treasure in it. |
| He began to lend money at interest to whomever he wished. | He built a great palace with it and passed through the bazaar with a train of slaves whom he had bought with that treasure. |

> When the seller saw it, he could
> have hanged himself (from anger).

Whereas in Matthew the parable of the Treasure describes how a man is overwhelmed with delight (see below p. 158), in the Gospel of Thomas, under the influence of the rabbinic story, the point is entirely lost: the parable now describes a man's anger at having failed to seize a unique opportunity.

The second instance, in which a folk-story theme has been introduced as a secondary element into a parable, occurs in Matthew. Into the parable of the Great Supper he has inserted the description of a punitive expedition: the king, enraged by the abuse and slaughter of his servants, sends out his bodyguard with orders to kill the murderers and burn their city (Matt. 22.7). This episode, which does not fit into the context (see p. 55) and is not in Luke or the Gospel of Thomas, makes use of a theme drawn from the ancient East and current in ancient Judaism; in Matt. 22.7 it reflects the destruction of Jerusalem.

## 5 The Change of Audience

The *parable of the Labourers in the Vineyard* (Matt. 20.1–16) affords a good example of the frequently occurring change of audience. To realize the various interpretations that it has undergone, we shall move backwards as regards time.

(*a*) In the Roman, Lutheran, and Anglican churches this parable is read on Septuagesima Sunday, i.e. at the beginning of the time of repentance before the Passion. The corresponding Epistle is I Cor. 9.24–27, the summons to run the Christian race. What does the Church preach at the beginning of the time of repentance? The call to God's vineyard. From the earliest times this has been very much allegorized: from so long ago as the time of Irenaeus (*c.* AD 150) the hours of the fivefold summons have been taken to symbolize the periods in the history of redemption from

Adam onwards; from Origen's time (AD 185–254) they have symbolized the different stages of life at which men become Christians. These two interpretations, from periods of human history and of human life, are often linked together. But, apart altogether from these allegorical interpretations, the parable does not bear the meaning of a summons to God's vineyard. Such an interpretation misses the point of the ending (vv. 8ff.), which shows that the stress is not on a call to the vineyard, but on the distribution of wages at the end of the day.

(*b*) Going further back, we find that all New Testament MSS., with the exception of the old Egyptian MSS. and translations, read as the concluding sentence of the parable, v. 16b, 'For many are called, but few are chosen'. How does the parable illustrate the truth that many are called but few are chosen—i.e., that only a few obtain salvation? The first, those who were summoned quite early, are here presented as a warning: they were called, but as they grumble, insist on their deserts, rebel against God's decision—in short, reject God's gift, as is often said—they cut themselves off from salvation. They are told to 'go' (v. 14). Here, then, the parable is understood as one of judgment: do not forfeit salvation by grumbling, self-righteousness, or rebellion. But this interpretation, too, misses the point. What the first labourers receive is not condemnation, but the agreed wage. It is not by accident that v. 16b is not in the early Egyptian MSS. and versions, which, generally, give us the best text. What we have here is one of those common generalizing conclusions, in this case taken from Matt. 22.14, and added not later than the second century.

(*c*) If we go back still further, we come to the evangelist Matthew himself. He has inserted into a Markan context the parable about the 'first' (Matt. 20.8, 10) and the 'last' (20.8, 12, 14) so as to illustrate the saying in Mark 10.31 (par. Matt. 19.30) 'But many that are first will be last, and the last first', with which Mark ends the preceding address to Peter. Transposing the order of 'first' and 'last', Matthew has used the saying again as the conclusion of the parable (Matt. 20.16), and twice, by the word 'for' (20.1) and by the word 'so' (20.16), expressly refers to 19.30. In the context according to Mark, this passage means that in God's world that is to come all earthly gradations of rank will be reversed; and it is uncertain whether it is intended to confirm the promises that Jesus has just made to the disciples, or to warn them against presumption. In either case, the parable illustrated for Matthew the reversal of rank on the day of judgment. He will have inferred this from the instruction given to the steward in v. 8b:

> 'Call the labourers and pay them their wages,
> beginning with the last, up to the first.'

The last became the first: it is with them that the payment of wages begins. Against this view, that the parable is intended to illustrate how on the last day the first will become last and the last first, it is not a valid objection that not merely two, but five groups are concerned, since from v. 8 onwards only the first- and last-mentioned groups are in evidence, the three intermediate groups being forgotten; these were mentioned only to illustrate the circumstances leading up to the engagement of labourers, especially the pressing need for labour. But we shall have to raise another objection to the view that the parable is intended to illustrate the final reversal of order on the last day. That view is based, as we have said, on v. 8b: 'beginning with the last, up to the first'. But that is clearly an unimportant detail of the parable. There can be no great significance in the order of payment; a couple of minutes earlier or later can hardly be a matter of discrimination either for or against anyone. In fact, no one complains later about the order of payment which, taken in its context, should merely emphasize the equality of the last with the first; or perhaps it is simply intended to indicate how 'the first witnessed the payment of their companions' (Jülicher). In any case, the parable certainly conveys no lesson about the reversal of rank at the end, since all receive exactly the same wage.

(*d*) Now, as Mark shows, the present Matthean context is not original, so we must go back behind Matthew and consider the parable without reference to its context. It thus becomes possible that the final sentence in v. 16 means something quite different from what its present Matthean setting demands. The seer of II (4) Esd. is perplexed by the question whether the preceding generations will be at a disadvantage compared with those who survive to the end, and he receives the answer: 'He said to me, "I shall liken my judgment to a circle; just as for those who are last there is no slowness, so for those who are first there is no haste" ' (II [4] Esd. 5.42). First and last, last and first—there is no difference; all are equal. This interpretation of the parable is generally accepted today: namely, that it is intended to teach the equality of reward in the Kingdom of God; some would add that it is intended to teach that all reward is wholly of grace; but this is erroneous, for the first received their pay, as Paul would say, 'not . . . as a gift but as his due' (Rom. 4.4). But apart from this, the point of the story, surprising to the hearers, is certainly not 'Equal pay for all', but 'Such high pay for the last!'

(*e*) The matter becomes clear if we disregard v. 16 ('So the last will be first, and the first last'). As is shown by Mark 10.31; Luke 13.30 (cf. Mark 9.35), this verse was originally an independent saying, perhaps nothing more than a proverb,[1] which has been added to our parable as a generalizing conclusion, but does not tally with its meaning. There are numerous examples of the insertion of such generalizing conclusions. But if the parable originally ended with the question in v. 15, without offering an explanation, its shocking character stares one in the face. Here is a story of obvious injustice. The double grievance (v. 12; see p. 109)

---

[1] Something like 'How easily fortune changes overnight'; cf. J. Schniewind, *Das Evangelium nach Markus*, Das Neue Testament Deutsch 1[11], Göttingen, 1963, on Mark 10.31.

is indeed only too well founded, and each hearer must have asked, 'Why does the master of the house give the unusual order that everyone is to have the same pay? Why especially does he give the last a full day's pay for only one hour's work? Is this injustice simply arbitrary? Is it caprice? A generous whim?' Far from it. There is no question here of unlimited generosity, for they all receive only an amount necessary to support life, a subsistence wage. No one gets more. Even if, in the case of the last labourers to be hired, it is their own fault that, even at the time of the vine-harvest, they sit about in the market-place gossiping till late afternoon, even if their excuse that no one has hired them (v. 7) is nothing but an idle evasion (like that of the servant in Matt. 25.24f.), a cover for their typical oriental in-difference, the owner is sorry for them. They will have prac-tically nothing to take home; the pay for an hour's work will not keep a family; their children will go hungry if the father comes home empty-handed. It is because of his pity for their poverty that the owner allows them to be paid a full day's wages. This means that the parable describes, not an arbitrary action, but the behaviour of a kindly man who is generous and full of sympathy for the poor. That, says Jesus, is how God deals with men. That is what God is like— merciful. Even to tax-collectors and sinners he grants an unmerited place in his kingdom, so great is his goodness. The whole emphasis is on the final words: 'my generosity' (v. 15).

Why did Jesus tell the parable? Was his object to extol God's mercy to the poor? In that case he might have left out the second part (vv. 8ff.). But it is precisely on the second part that the main stress lies, for our parable is one of the two-edged ones. It describes two episodes: (1) the hiring of the labourers and the liberal instructions about their payment (vv. 1–8); (2) the indignation of the recipients with a grievance (vv. 9–15). Now in all the two-edged parables the emphasis lies on the second part (see pp. 103f. on Luke 15.11ff.; p. 147 on Luke 16.19ff.; pp. 52f. on Matt. 22.1–14). Why, then, is there this second part, the episode in which

the other labourers are indignant, rise up in protest, and
receive the humiliating reply: 'Do you begrudge my
generosity?' (v. 15). The parable is clearly addressed to
those who resembled the grumblers, those who criticized the
good news and took offence at it—Pharisees, for example.
It was they whom Jesus wanted to show how unjustified,
hateful, loveless, and unmerciful their criticism was. That,
he told them, is what God is like—so kind! And because
God is so kind, so am I. He vindicates the gospel against
its critics. Here we have evidently recovered the original
historical setting. We are suddenly taken into a concrete
situation in Jesus' life, such as the Gospels frequently
describe. Over and over again we hear the charge brought
against him that he is a companion of the despised and
outcast, and are told of people to whom the gospel is an
offence. He repeatedly has to justify his conduct and
vindicate the good news. So here, too, he is saying: That is
what God is like, so very kind, so full of compassion for the
poor. Are you going to censure him?

As the context in Matthew (Peter's question in 19.27)
shows, the primitive Church related the parable to Jesus'
disciples, and so applied it to the Christian community.
That is easy to understand, for it was in the same position
as the Church is today when it preaches about the Pharisee-
stories of the Gospels—it has to apply to the community
words that were addressed to opponents. Thus we have
gained a method of approach to the parables which is of
far-reaching significance, an additional principle of transformation, namely: the tradition underwent a change or
restriction of the audience. Many parables which were
originally addressed to a different audience, namely the
Pharisees, the scribes, or the crowd, were subsequently
connected with Jesus' disciples by the primitive Church.

One more example out of a great number of similar cases
may be mentioned: Luke 15.3–7 par. Matt. 18.12–14.
According to Luke, the *parable of the Lost Sheep* was
occasioned by the Pharisees' indignant protest that 'this man

receives sinners and eats with them' (15.2), and it closes (in
Luke) with the words, 'Even so, I tell you, there will be more
joy in heaven [at the last judgment][1] over one sinner who
repents than over ninety-nine righteous persons who need
no repentance' (15.7). It was with the object of justifying the
gospel against its critics that Jesus asserted, through a
parable, that just as a shepherd, gathering his flock into the
fold, rejoices over the lost sheep that he has found, so God
rejoices over the repentant sinner. He rejoices because he can
forgive. That, says Jesus, is why I receive sinners.[2]

In Matthew the parable has an entirely different audience.
According to 18.1 it is not addressed, as in Luke, to Jesus'
opponents, but to his disciples; and accordingly the final
sentence in Matthew has a different emphasis. It runs: 'So
it is not the will of my Father who is in heaven that one of
these little ones should perish' (18.14). In the context of the
admonition not to despise 'one of these little ones' (v. 10),
and of the instruction concerning the discipline of an
erring brother (vv. 15–17), the concluding sentence clearly
means: It is God's will that you should go after your back-
sliding brother—especially the 'little', the weak, the helpless
—as faithfully as the shepherd in the parable seeks the lost
sheep. Thus, in Matthew the parable is addressed to the
disciples, and calls on the leaders of the community to act
as faithful shepherds towards those who fall away; the
emphasis does not lie, as in Luke, on the shepherd's joy, but
on the example of his persistent search. But the great
instruction given in Matt. 18 to the leaders of the churches
(for this is the chapter's intention, the usual interpretation of
it as an instruction to the community being incorrect), in
the context of which the Matthean parable stands, is a
secondary composition, an expansion of the collection of
sayings in Mark 9.33–50 (which are linked by catchword
association). So the Matthean context does not help us to
determine the original situation that led Jesus to tell the

[1] It is generally overlooked that the statement refers to the future.
[2] See pp. 107f.

parable of the Lost Sheep. There can be no doubt that Luke has preserved the original situation. As in so many other instances, we have Jesus vindicating the good news against its critics, and declaring God's character, God's delight in forgiveness, as the reason why he himself received sinners.

Thus we find the same process as in Matt. 20.1–16—a parable originally directed at Jesus' opponents (in Luke) has become one addressed to the disciples (in Matthew). The change of audience has meant a shift of emphasis: justification has been turned into exhortation.

The fact that the statements about the audience, which, of course, belong to the parables' setting, and were therefore more open to variation than the parables themselves, need to be carefully examined, is confirmed by the realization that on occasion the Gospels are contradictory on this point. Thus, in Matthew the parable of the Lost Sheep (18.12–14), and in Mark the simile of the salt (9.50), are addressed to the disciples; but according to Luke the first is addressed to Jesus' opponents (15.2), and the second to the crowd (14.25). A detailed analysis of the statements about the people who heard the parables (beyond the two examples examined above, pp. 24–31) shows that, in the transmission of the Gospels' material, a strong tendency was at work to turn parables that Jesus addressed to the crowd or to opponents, into parables for the disciples—a tendency characteristic of all three synoptic evangelists. I do not know of any case where the reverse process can be proved—where a parable addressed to the disciples was converted into one addressed to the crowd.

We must therefore always ask who were the original hearers, and what a parable means if we take it as addressed to opponents or the crowd.

## 6  *The Hortatory Use of the Parables by the Church*

In studying the parable of the Lost Sheep, we saw that Jesus originally used it to defend the gospel against his opponents, but that Matthew put it into the setting of the disciplinary order of the community as an exhortation to its leaders to be faithful in their pastoral duties. In other words, the parable lost its first historical setting, and, as often happened, was used by the Church solely as hortatory material.

The little *parable about Going before the Judge* has been handed down to us in Matthew (5.25f.) and in Luke (12.58f.), with essential agreement in content, in spite of minor verbal differences. But the two evangelists have put the parable into very different settings. In Matthew it is connected with the first antithesis of the Sermon on the Mount, the prohibition of hate (5.21f.). It is better to be reconciled, is the advice of vv. 23f., otherwise your worship is a sham; not till you have been reconciled will God accept your offering and your prayer for forgiveness. But suppose the dispute has now reached the stage of legal proceedings, possibly over the amount due to the creditor? In that case, says the Matthean form of the parable, you should go to all lengths to reach an agreement with your opponent. Give way! Take the first step! Come to terms! Otherwise there is danger ahead. Anyone who stands implacably on his supposed rights may come to grief on legal grounds. So in Matthew the parable is regarded as a direction for the conduct of life, and there is no denying that the motive behind this direction sounds dangerously near triviality.

In Luke the parable has a very different context. It follows a series of sayings (from 12.35 on) that refer to the impending crisis and the signs of the times. Jesus severely rebukes the people for their failure to realize the gravity of the present moment (12.56f.). In this connection the parable of the Debtor bears a different emphasis from that which it bears in Matthew. In Luke the whole stress is on the present danger to the defendant. He is told: 'You are about to stand before the judge, and you are threatened with condemnation and imprisonment. You may be arrested at any moment: act at once while you are still at liberty, and settle the matter while it is still possible!' There can be no doubt that Luke is right; the parable is an eschatological one, a parable of crisis. The crisis is at the door, and is the turning-point of history. The last chance must be seized, before it is too late.

The divergence between the two evangelists reveals a characteristic shift of emphasis. Luke emphasizes God's eschatological action; Matthew, the disciples' conduct. Jesus lived in expectation of the great catastrophe, the final temptation (Mark 14.38), the last crisis of history which his death would introduce. Increasingly, as time went on, the primitive Church saw itself midway between two crises, one belonging to the past, and the other to the future. Standing thus between the cross and Christ's return, the Church looked to Jesus' guidance, and found itself forced by the changed conditions to interpret those of his parables which were intended to rouse people to a sense of the gravity of the moment, as directions for the conduct of the Christian community; in theological language, the stress moved from the eschatological to the hortatory. At the same time, this did not eliminate the eschatological content of Jesus' sayings, but 'actualized' it (A. Vögtle) by stressing the need for reconciliation.

The *parable of the Great Supper* in the Gospel of Thomas 64 ends with the sentence, 'Tradesmen and merchants shall not enter the places of my Father.' Even if the reference is, in the first place, to the well-to-do people who decline the invitation, its generalized terms convey the idea of a sharp attack on the rich. This attitude of class-consciousness is to some extent in line with that of Luke, who makes the parable (14.16–24) follow the admonition (14.12–14) not to invite people of wealth and good standing, but 'the poor, the maimed, the lame, the blind'. By the repetition of this list in 14.21 he indicates that the parable is intended to be an example of 14.12–14: one should behave like the house-holder in the parable, who symbolically invites to his table the poor, the lame, the blind, and the halt. But that is surely not the parable's original intention; in it, as we shall see later, Jesus is rather justifying to his critics the preaching of the good news to the poor: he is saying, in effect, 'While you are refusing salvation, God is calling the despised to share in the salvation of his people'. In Luke the story has been transformed from a vindication into a call to do like-wise. The emphasis has again moved from the eschatological to the admonitory.

We shall meet with many examples of this change of emphasis; a typical case is in the *parable of the Unjust Steward* (Luke 16.1ff.), which, for reasons that are not far to seek, has been expanded several times. It is a debatable question who is meant by *kyrios*, 'master' in v. 8 ('The master commended the dishonest steward'). The change of subject ('And I tell you') at the beginning of v. 9 seems to point decisively to the conclusion that it means the 'master' in the parable (vv. 3, 5). According to this view the application of the parable comes in v. 9: as the unjust steward cancelled debts so that the debtors might receive him into their houses (v. 4), Jesus' disciples are to use the unrighteous mammon so that the angels (see p. 35 n. 1) may receive them 'into the eternal habitations' (v. 9). But it is doubtful whether this was the parable's original meaning. It is difficult to see how the 'master' of v. 8 can refer to the lord in the parable; how could he have praised his deceitful steward? Above all, the analogy of 18.6 suggests that the 'master' is Jesus, since it is plain that here with the words 'And the Lord (*kyrios*) said' the judgment of Jesus is inserted into a parable; and yet there occurs here, too, in 18.8, his 'I tell you'. But if the 'master' of 16.8 originally referred to Jesus, we may infer that between vv. 8 and 9 there is a join, which is explained by the fact that several sayings (vv. 9–13) marked by the term 'mammon' (vv. 9, 11, 13) have been added to the parable.

The recognition of this fact enables us to analyse the section Luke 16.1–13 as follows: (1) The parable (vv. 1–7) describes a criminal who, when threatened with exposure, adopts unscrupulous but resolute measures to ensure his future security. In v. 8a we get Jesus' application of the parable—he 'commended the dishonest steward for his prudence'. The man's clever and resolute behaviour when he was threatened by catastrophe is to be an example to Jesus' hearers. (In v. 8b this surprising commendation is explained: rightly understood, it is limited to the children of this world in their dealings with one another, and not in relation to God.) (2) In v. 9 we have an entirely different application of the parable from that which is given in 8a: 'Make friends[1] for yourselves by means of unrighteous mammon, so that when it fails they may receive you into the eternal habitations.'[2] (This saying, which has been brought into connection with the parable through verbal association, must originally have been addressed to tax-collectors or others classed as dishonest people.) Even on this interpretation, the steward is held up as an example, not because of his prudent resolution, when threatened with disaster, to make a fresh start for himself, but because of his wise use of illegally obtained money: he used it to help others. (Indeed, we may wonder whether this was really in the parable at all.) (3) But is the man really an example to be followed? In vv. 10–12, which are connected with v. 9 by the words 'dishonest' (v. 10) and 'unrighteous mammon' (v. 11), we have a third interpretation of the parable in the form of a proverb composed of two antithetic terms (v. 10) dealing with faithfulness and unfaithfulness in very little things, and in vv. 11–12 applied to mammon and ever-lasting riches. On this third interpretation the steward is not an example to be followed, but an awful warning—the

[1] The 'friends' may well be the angels, i.e. God (cf. v. 9b, where the third person plural refers to the angels—i.e. is used as a circumlocution for God).

[2] Living in 'tents' or 'booths' is a feature of the eschatological consummation: Mark 9.5; Acts 15.16; Rev. 7.15; 21.3.

parable being understood by contraries. (4) An originally isolated saying (v. 13), attached, as Matt. 6.24 shows, to the word 'mammon', closes the section with a sharp contrast between the service of God and the service of mammon, and calls for a decision between the two.

Thus the parable's interpretation has to come simply from v. 8a. If, as v. 8a suggests, it is a summons to resolute action in a crisis, it would hardly have been addressed to the disciples, but rather to the 'unconverted', the hesitant, the waverers, the crowd. These are the people who are to hear the call—the all-decisive turning-point is just ahead, and they must be urged to act bravely, wisely, and resolutely, to stake all on the future. The primitive Church applied the parable to the Christian community (Luke 16.1, 'to his disciples'; v. 9, 'you'), and drew from it a direction for the right use of wealth, and a warning against unfaithfulness—i.e. shifted the emphasis from the eschatological to the admonitory.

It would, however, be wrong to infer that through this change of emphasis the primitive Church introduced an entirely foreign element into the parable. Even in its original form it contains an implied exhortation, for Jesus' command to be resolute and make a fresh start embraces the generosity of v. 9, the faithfulness of vv. 10–12, and the rejection of mammon in v. 13; thus the parable is merely 'actualized'. It would also be wrong to infer that the primitive Church completely banished the eschatological element from the parable, for it was the Church's eschatological situation that lent weight to its exhortations. It is not a matter of adding or taking away, but of a shift of emphasis resulting from a change of audience.

## 7 The Influence of the Church's Situation

(a) *The Delay in Christ's Return*
The realization that the primitive Church related the parables to its own concrete situation, and by so doing produced a

shift of emphasis, is, as C. H. Dodd pointed out, of fundamental importance for the understanding of the five
*Parousia* parables. Let us first examine the little *parable of
the Burglar* (Matt. 24.43f.; Luke 12.39f.). 'But know this,
that if the householder had known in what part of the night
[Luke: at what hour] the thief was coming, he would have
watched and [the last four words are not in the original
Greek text of Luke] would not have let his house be broken
into. Therefore you also must be ready; for the Son of man
is coming at an hour you do not expect.' The situation described in the parable is clear. Jesus draws upon an actual
happening, some recent burglary about which the whole
village is talking. He uses this exciting occurrence as a
warning of the catastrophe that he sees approaching. Be on
your guard, he says, that you may not be caught unawares
like this man the other day by the burglary. Yet the application of the parable to the return of the Son of man is
strange. Referring as it does to a nocturnal raid, its subject
is an unpleasant and frightening occurrence, whereas the
*Parousia* is the great day of joy, at least for Jesus' disciples.
With this in mind we shall not be surprised to find that the
application is lacking in the Gospel of Thomas. Here the
parable of the Burglar has been preserved in two versions;
one of them (21b) resembles the text of Matthew, the other
(103) is a free reproduction which has been cast into the
form of a beatitude and shows some affinity to Luke 12.35ff.
Both versions agree in the fact that the application of the
burglar to the returning Son of man is lacking. If we disregard it, the nearest parallels to our parable are to be
found in the parables of the Deluge (Matt. 24.37–39;
Luke 17.26f.) and of the Rain of Fire (Luke 17.28–32). Here,
too, events, although of extreme antiquity, which overwhelmed men unprepared, are used by Jesus as a warning
of terrors to come. He sees disaster draw near, the catastrophe is at the door; indeed, with his coming it has already
broken in—and the people round him are as heedless as the
householder; they pass their days, like those before the

flood and the rain of fire, just as if there were no danger. Jesus wants to rouse them, to open their eyes to the danger that they are in. Terror is drawing near, as unexpected as the housebreaker, as terrible as the deluge. Prepare yourselves! Soon it will be too late. That is how Jesus' hearers must have understood the parable of the Burglar—as an urgent warning to the crowd in view of the imminent eschatological catastrophe.

The primitive Church applied the parable to its members (Luke 12.22 'to his disciples'; Matt. 24.3). Indeed, Luke specially emphasizes that it concerns only the apostles, the responsible leaders of the community, for Peter's ensuing question, 'Lord, are you telling this parable for us or for all?' (Luke 12.41) is answered in the former sense by the parable of the steward who is put to the test by the delay in his master's return (Luke 12.42–48): It is told to you, because you have a special responsibility. Thus the parable becomes a summons to the leaders of the Church, in view of the delay in Christ's return, not to become slack; and with the help of Christological allegorizing, the burglar becomes a figure representing the Son of man.

To sum up, then, we may say that the parable of the Burglar was applied by the Church to its own changed situation, which was characterized by the delay of Christ's return, and that the result was a somewhat changed emphasis. No doubt its eschatological character was preserved, but the warning to the crowd became an admonition to the Christian community and its leaders; the proclamation of the coming catastrophe became a direction as to conduct in view of the delay in Christ's return, and by means of an allegorical interpretation the parable received a Christological twist.

Here we must guard carefully against a misunderstanding. The fact that Jesus related the parable of the Burglar to the impending catastrophe does not mean that his return lay outside the field of vision. On the other hand, the fact that the early Church related it to his return does not mean that they knew nothing of the

impending catastrophe. On the contrary, as to eschatological
expectation there is no difference between Jesus and the early
Church; both expected that the first stage of the crisis would be
marked by the sudden irruption of the time of tribulation and the
revelation of satanic power over the whole earth; and both—
Jesus and the Church—were convinced that this last tribulation
would end with the triumph of God. The difference was simply
that Jesus, speaking to the crowd, emphasized the sudden irruption of the tribulation (Be ready, for the tribulation will overtake
you as unexpectedly as the thief's invasion), whereas the early
Church's gaze was directed to the end of the tribulation (Do
not cease to be watchful, for the Lord's return will be as unexpected as the breaking-in of a thief).

Matthew's understanding of the *parable of the Ten
Maidens* (25.1–13), belonging to his special material, is
shown by the context (24.32–25.46 are clearly *Parousia*-
parables), as well as by vv. 1 and 13. In v. 1 the 'then' refers
back to the 'coming' mentioned in 24.44 and 50, and this is
also referred to in v. 13: 'Watch therefore, for you know
neither the day nor the hour.' Thus Matthew saw in the
parable an allegory of the return of Christ, the heavenly
bridegroom: the ten maidens are the expectant Christian
community, the 'delaying' of the bridegroom (v. 5) is the
postponement of the return, his sudden coming (v. 6) is the
unexpected return of Christ himself, and the stern rejection
of the foolish maidens (v. 11) is the final judgment. Moreover,
it seems that quite early the foolish maidens were supposed
to represent Israel, and the wise maidens the Gentiles; at any
rate the Lukan tradition sees in the refusal of admittance to
those who knocked too late at the door (Luke 13.25) the
rejection of Israel at the last judgment.

But was all this the parable's original meaning? In
answering this question we shall have to disregard the
Matthean context, as well as the 'then' (v. 1), which is one
of Matthew's favourite and characteristic transition par-
ticles. We must also disregard v. 13, for this concluding
admonition to watch misses the parable's meaning. They all

slept, the wise maidens as well as the foolish (v. 5). What is blamed is not the sleeping, but the failure of the foolish maidens to provide oil for their lamps. Thus the exhortation to watchfulness in v. 13 is one of those admonitory additions that people liked to make to the parables; it repeats Matt. 24.42, and belonged originally to the parable of the Door-keeper (Mark 13.35). The references to Christ's return, therefore, do not belong to the original form of the parable. Further, it is open to doubt whether Matt. 25.1–12 was originally an allegory, for the allegorical picture of the Messiah as a bridegroom is quite foreign to the Old Testament and to Late Judaism; it appears for the first time in Paul's writings (II Cor. 11.2). Jesus' audience could hardly have thought of applying the figure of the bridegroom in Matt. 25.1ff. to the Messiah. As this allegory is also absent from the rest of Jesus' preaching,[1] we must conclude that Matt. 25.1ff. is not an allegory about Christ the heavenly bridegroom, but that Jesus was telling of an actual wedding. At the most the parable conceals a messianic utterance of Jesus which only his disciples could understand.

How then must his audience have understood the parable, especially if we regard the audience as consisting of the crowd, as Luke 13.22–30 suggests? The sudden coming of the bridegroom (v. 6) has its parallels in the sudden down-pour of the flood, the unexpected entry of the thief, and the unlooked-for return of the master of the house from the feast or journey. In all these it is suddenness which charac-terizes the unexpected catastrophe. The crisis is at the door.

---

[1] Nor is the allegory of the bridegroom as the Messiah to be found in Mark 2.19a (Matt. 9.15a; Luke 5.34). For the subordinate clause 'as long as the bridegroom is with them' may originally have been another way of saying 'during the wedding'. To the question why his disciples did not fast, Jesus replied with the counter-question, 'Can the wedding-guests fast during the wedding?' It would be just as meaningless for the disciples to fast who are already in full enjoyment of the new age. The allegory of the bridegroom as the Messiah does not appear till Mark 2.20 (Matt. 9.15b; Luke 5.35). But this verse, which contradicts Mark 2.19a by declaring that a time will come for Jesus' disciples to fast, is certainly a product of the early Church.

It will come as unexpectedly as the midnight cry in the parable, 'Behold, the bridegroom!' And it brings the inexorable separation, even where mortal eyes see no distinction (cf. Matt. 24.40f.; Luke 17.34f.; Gospel of Thomas 61a). Woe to those whom that hour finds unprepared! Thus it was as a cry of warning in view of the imminent eschatological crisis that Jesus uttered the parable, and as such the crowd understood it.

The early Church interpreted the bridegroom as Christ, and his midnight coming as the *Parousia*, the second coming of Christ. This did not deviate from the original meaning in so far as the eschatological catastrophe and Christ's second coming are, in fact, two aspects of the same event (see pp. 38f.); in spite of the Christological interpretation of the bridegroom, the coming separation of the wise and the foolish maidens was still the aim and central point of the text. And yet an essential change of emphasis took place: the warning cry intended to awake the crowd from sleep became an exhortation to the band of disciples, and the parable became an allegory of Christ the heavenly bridegroom and the Church that awaited him.

The third of the *Parousia*-parables to be discussed is the *parable of the Doorkeeper* (Mark 13.33–37; Luke 12.35–38; cf. Matt. 24.42). It shows unusually wide variations in the three Synoptics; it has been very much used, and, under the influence of the *Parousia*-motive, worked over and expanded—showing how important to the primitive Church was the exhortation to watchfulness. Starting with Luke 12.35–38, we are first of all struck by the rewarding of the watchful servants: 'Truly, I say to you, he [the master of the house] will gird himself and have them sit at table, and he will come and serve them' (12.37b). No earthly master behaves like that (cf. Luke 17.7), but Jesus has done so (Luke 22.27; John 13.4–5); and he will do so again on his return. Verse 37b is therefore an allegorizing detail, which disturbs the setting of the parable, breaks the connection between v. 37a and v. 38, and refers to the messianic banquet at Christ's return. A second detail in Luke is noteworthy: while in Mark it is only the doorkeeper—as befits his office—who is told to watch till his master returns, in Luke it is a number of servants, evidently all of them, who are to watch; here, too, the application of the parable to the whole Christian community undoubtedly made its imprint on the text.

The Markan version of the parable (13.33–37) is original in so far as the command to watch is addressed only to the doorkeeper (v. 34b). But it has secondary features in two places through the influence of related parables. The words 'like a man going on a journey' (v. 34) may well come from the parable of the Talents (Matt. 25.14), since the order to the doorkeeper to keep watch during the night, while it is in keeping with an invitation to the master of the house to attend a banquet (Luke 12.36) which may last far into the night, does not, on the other hand, suit a longer journey with no date of return fixed, and from which, moreover, in view of the oriental aversion to night journeys, a return by night is unlikely. As in the case of the 'man going on a journey', so too the transfer of authority to the servants (Mark 13.34) is out of place in the parable of the Doorkeeper. It is derived from the parable of the Servant entrusted with Supervision (Matt. 24.45; Luke 12.42), which is concerned with the conscientious administration of what is entrusted to him during his master's prolonged absence; a householder who has merely accepted an invitation hardly needs to assign special powers to his servants. Finally, in Matthew the parable has disappeared, and only the application remains: 'Watch therefore, for you do not know on what day your Lord is coming' (24.42; cf. 25.13). If we compare Mark 13.35: 'Watch therefore—for you do not know when the master of the house will come, in the evening, or at midnight, or at cockcrow, or in the morning', we see that 'the master of the house' has become 'your Lord', and that the night-watch has become the day—the Christological interpretation is obvious; it occurs not only in Matt. 24.42 and Luke

12.37b, but also in Rev. 3.20, and thus spread rapidly throughout the whole Church.

We are thus left with a core consisting of the parable of the Doorkeeper, who had been told to keep watch (Mark 13.34b) and to open at once when his master, coming home from the banquet, should knock (Luke 12.36). It would be well for him if his master found him watching, in whatever watch of the night he returned (Luke 12.37a, 38; Mark 13.35f.). What had Jesus in mind, and to what audience did he address his call to watchfulness? If he was speaking to his disciples, we may compare the appeal to watch in Gethsemane: 'Watch and pray that you may not enter into temptation' (Mark 14.38), when he was thinking of the final temptation, the beginning of the eschatological tribulation, Satan's attack on the saints of God, which he expected to be ushered in by his passion. But if Jesus was speaking to the crowd, then we may compare the parable about the flood: calamity is impending, as unpredictable as the return of the householder! Be watchful! It seems to me most likely that the parable of the Doorkeeper was addressed to those who claimed to possess the keys of the Kingdom of Heaven (Matt. 23.13; Luke 11.52)—that is, to the scribes: take care not to be found asleep when the decisive moment comes! Whoever the original hearers were, it is plain that we have here a crisis-parable, and that if it contains a messianic utterance of Jesus about himself, it is, at the most, a concealed one. The primitive Church applied the parable to its own situation, lying between two crises and awaiting the delayed return of Christ. It therefore expanded the parable by adding a series of new, allegorizing features: now the master of the house is going on a long journey (Mark); he tells all his servants to watch (Luke), he gives them authority before he leaves home (Mark), the day (not the night-watch) of his return is uncertain (Matthew), the reward that he gives is selfless service to his own at the messianic banquet (Luke).

A very similar fate has befallen the closely related *parable of the Servant entrusted with Supervision*—for so we must describe it, as it speaks of one servant, not two (Matt. 24.45–51; Luke 12.41–46). This servant was given a position of trust, and his master's unexpected return from a journey would show whether he was worthy of the trust, or whether he had been tempted by his master's delayed return to abuse his power by terrorizing his fellow-servants and by self-indulgence. In Matthew and Luke, as is shown by the context (Matt. 24.44; Luke 12.40) and by the mention of the punishment of hell (Matt. 24.51bc; Luke 12.46c), the 'master' in the parable has been interpreted as the Son of man returning to judge the world, and the parable has been understood as an admonition to Jesus' disciples not to weaken in their trust because of the delay in Christ's return. The tradition underlying Luke has gone a step further: influenced by the granting of authority to the servant over his fellows, it has regarded this servant as representing the apostles (Luke 12.41), and has applied the parable solely to them. The passage in 12.47f., peculiar to Luke, adds that a great responsibility has been entrusted to them; they know the Master's will better than others, and more has been given to them than to others; hence a sterner reckoning will be demanded of them if they allow the delay in Christ's return to cause them to abuse their office. But we can hardly discern the parable's original intention in these applications of it by Matthew and Luke. In the story no stress is laid on the delay in the master's return; the words 'My master is delayed' (Matt. 24.48; Luke 12.45) are originally intended simply to bring out the temptation involved in the position in which the servant found himself. The object is rather to emphasize the sudden test to which his conduct was exposed.

If we want to find out the parable's original meaning, we must again ask how the picture of the servant, distinguished by a special position of trust and responsibility, suddenly tested by his master's unexpected return, would have affected Jesus' audience. From the Old Testament they were familiar with the designation of leaders, rulers, prophets, and sacred persons, as 'servants of God'; they regarded the scribes as overseers whom God had appointed and to whom he had entrusted the keys of the Kingdom of Heaven (Matt. 23.13; Luke 11.52); and they would therefore see in the responsible servant of the parable the religious leaders of their time. When this is recognized, the parable falls into close relationship with the situation of the life of Jesus. It is seen to be one of his many stern warnings to the leaders of the people, especially to the scribes, that the day of reckoning was at hand, when God would reveal whether they had been faithful to the trust committed to them, or had abused it.

It is understandable that the primitive Church interpreted the tarrying of the master of the house as the delaying of Christ's return; it saw the householder as the Son of man who had departed to heaven and would suddenly return to judge the world; the servant was interpreted as the members, or (in Luke) the leaders, of the Christian community, who were exhorted not to allow themselves to be led into temptation while waiting for Christ's return.

A more detailed counterpart of this parable is the *parable of the Talents*. It has come to us in three versions: Matt. 25.14–30; Luke 19.12–27; and in the Gospel of the Nazarenes. Let us work backwards from the version that has diverged most widely from the original. In the Gospel of the Nazarenes[1] there appears, as well as the servant who multiplied the money entrusted to him, and the one who hid his talent, a third servant who squandered the money on harlots and flute-players; the first is commended, the second rebuked, and the third thrown into prison. This version, which puts the mark of unfaithfulness only on extravagance (cf. Luke 15.30; 12.45), is a moralistic simplification which the

[1] The Aramaic Gospel of the Nazarenes, of which only fragments now remain, may have originated in the first half of the second century. In essentials it goes back to the Greek Gospel by Matthew; but it also has material derived from old tradition. What is left of the Nazarene version of the parable of the Talents can be found in M. R. James, *The Apocryphal New Testament*, Oxford, 1924 = 1953, p. 3 (under the erroneous heading, 'The Gospel according to the Hebrews').

parable underwent in the Jewish Christian Church. In Luke
as compared with Matthew the parable has a very different
aspect. Matthew's merchant is replaced by Luke's nobleman
who goes on a journey to claim a kingdom (v. 12); his
fellow-citizens try to frustrate his purpose by sending a
deputation after him (v. 14); but he returns as king (v. 15a;
cf. also the 'cities' in vv. 17 and 19), and has his enemies
slaughtered before his eyes (v. 27). In these features we may
possibly have a second, originally independent, *parable
about a Claimant to the Throne*, reflecting the historical
situation of 4 BC. At the time Archelaus journeyed to Rome
to get his kingship over Judaea confirmed; at the same time
a Jewish embassy of fifty persons also went to Rome to
resist his appointment. The bloody revenge inflicted on the
people by Archelaus after his return had never been forgotten, and Jesus seems to have used this occurrence in a
crisis-parable as a warning against a false sense of security.
Just as unexpectedly as the return and vengeance of
Archelaus overtook his opponents, so unexpectedly will
destruction overtake you.

The pre-Lukan tradition had already fused this parable
with our parable. The join is particularly obvious in vv. 24f.;
the additional rewarding of the first servant with one mina
(= 100 denarii), and the bystanders' objection that he
already has ten minas (= 1000 denarii) are meaningless,
after he has been appointed ruler over ten cities. To provide
a setting for the conflated parable, an introduction (19.11)
has been prefixed, stating that the parable was related in
order to refute false expectations that God's reign was to
appear at once. So we can see how Luke interpreted it:
Jesus, seeing that the second coming was eagerly expected,
announces that it is to be delayed, and explains the reason—
namely, that the intervening period is to be a testing-time
for the disciples. Luke therefore saw in the nobleman who
received a kingdom and on his return demanded a reckoning
from his servants, the Son of man departing to heaven and
returning to judgment. But Luke is certainly wrong. For

Jesus certainly did not compare himself, either with a man 'taking up where I did not lay down and reaping what I did not sow' (Luke 19.21)—that is, a rapacious man ruthlessly intent on his own profit—or with a brutal oriental despot, gloating over his enemies slaughtered before his eyes (v. 27). A comparison of details shows that Matthew has kept the earliest version, although even here secondary features can be seen.[1] Matthew, too, has interpreted the parable as a *Parousia*-parable (as we saw above that Luke has done—incorrectly!), since he has put it among the *Parousia*-parables, 24.32–25.13 and 25.31–46. The 'for' of the introduction (25.14) shows that it must have been intended to reinforce the exhortation to watchfulness in view of the unknown hour of the return. Matthew has been influenced by the Christological interpretation in two places in the parable: in the expression 'Enter into the joy of your master' (vv. 21, 23) and in the command to cast the unprofitable servant 'into the outer darkness' (v. 30). In both cases it is not an earthly merchant who is speaking, but the Christ who has returned, who awards a share in the New Age, and condemns men to eternal damnation. Neither of these features is in keeping with the original situation: we may infer this for vv. 21, 23 by comparing with Luke, where the reward remains in an earthly setting; and the minatory words in v. 30 (not in Luke) also break through the bounds of the parable's earthly setting, and by exhibiting the stylistic peculiarities of Matthew, as well as by the fact that they double the penalty by adding to the earthly penalty (v. 28) the punishment of hell, they reveal editorial activity.

If we discard these moralizing and allegorizing expansions, we have the story of a rich man, feared by his servants as an inconsiderate and rapacious employer, who, before setting out on a journey, entrusts to each of the three the sum of

---

[1] In Matthew the servants are entrusted with very large amounts, and must therefore be thought of as governors of some kind; in Luke, they are not appointed as such till after the reckoning. It is evident that the more modest sum of 100 denarii each, mentioned by Luke, is original (see p. 19).

100 denarii to be traded with—either merely so as not to
leave his capital unemployed during his absence, or so as to
test his servants—and accounted for on his return. The two
faithful servants are rewarded with increased responsibility.
The emphasis lies on the reckoning with the third servant,
who makes the lame excuse that, from an excess of caution,
he has made no use of the money entrusted to him, because
he knew his master's rapacity and feared lest, through the
failure of his business transactions, he might incur his
master's extreme anger at the loss of his money. According
to Luke, the servant behaved with inexcusable irresponsi-
bility; for while, according to Matt. 25.18, he had at least
taken the precaution of burying the money, according to
Luke 19.20 he had wrapped it in a napkin (this would be a
linen head-cloth of about one square yard), and so neglected
the most elementary safety precautions.[1] How would Jesus'
hearers understand the parable? What, in particular, would
they think about the servant who buried his talent? Did they
think of the Jewish people, to whom so much had been
entrusted, but who had not made use of their trust? Did
they think of the Pharisees, who sought to ensure their
personal salvation by a scrupulous observance of the law,
while by their selfish exclusiveness they made religion
sterile? We have already seen that his hearers would think,
in the first place, of their religious leaders, especially the
scribes. As Jesus reproached them (Luke 11.52) for with-
holding from their fellow-men their due share of God's gift,
we may take it that it was they to whom he originally
addressed the parable of the Talents. Much had been entrusted to them: the Word of God;[2] but, like the servants in

[1] According to rabbinical law, burying (Matt. 25.18) was regarded as
the best security against theft. Anyone who buried a pledge or a deposit
as soon as he received it was freed from liability. On the other hand, if
anyone tied up entrusted money in a cloth, he was responsible for making good any loss incurred through inadequate care of the deposit. It
should be noted that both Matthew and Luke presuppose Palestinian
conditions.

[2] For a comparison of the divine Word with a deposit entrusted by
God, cf. also I Tim. 6.20; II Tim. 1.12, 14.

the parable, they would soon have to give an account of how they had used what had been committed to them—whether they had used it in accordance with God's will, or whether, like the third servant, they had been 'making void the word of God' (Mark 7.13) by their self-seeking and their wanton neglect of God's gift.

Again the primitive Church applied this parable in various ways to its own actual situation. The beginning of this development can be seen in the fact that the command 'Take the pound from him, and give it to him who has the ten pounds' (Luke 19.24; cf. Matt. 25.28) is confirmed by the generalizing explanatory comment: 'I tell you, that to every one who has will more be given;[1] but from him who has not, even what he has will be taken away.'[2] The saying is an entirely relevant explanation of the command; the industrious servant's reward is, in fact, increased, while what the lazy servant has is taken away from him. Yet the addition of the explanatory comment changes the whole outlook; its insertion just before the final sentence makes it an interpretation of the whole parable, and not for one single verse (Matt. 25.28 par.). The main emphasis is now transferred to a secondary feature (v. 28), and so the parable becomes an exposition of the nature and manner of divine retribution. It seems unjust to make the rich man still richer, and to deprive the poor man of his last penny; and Luke makes the audience openly express surprise at such treatment—'Lord, he has ten pounds' (Luke 19.25). But the primitive Christian teaching affirms that this is what God's justice is like, and that it is therefore the more urgent to do our utmost to avoid failure. In the Gospel of the Nazarenes the hortatory element is even more obviously stressed: the parable has become a warning to the community against riotous living.

With this application of the parable, however, another tendency

[1] The passive forms 'will be given', 'will be taken away' are circumlocutions for the divine name; see p. 11 n. 2.

[2] Matt. 25.29 (par. Luke 19.26) breaks the connection between vv. 28 and 30; it is originally an isolated saying (Mark 4.25; Matt. 13.12; Luke 8.18; Gospel of Thomas 41) which was added to the parable as a generalizing conclusion (see pp. 85f.), and, as the agreement between Matthew and Luke shows, figured as such already in the tradition underlying both Gospels. It was perhaps originally a proverb: Life is like that—unjust.

soon appeared: its application to the delay of Christ's return, and the accompanying allegorization. The merchant's journey and continued absence, first mentioned only to explain why the servants were in charge of his money, become more and more the central point of the story. In Matthew the merchant has become an allegory of Christ, his journey has become the ascension, and his return 'after a long time' (Matt. 25.19) has become Christ's second coming, ushering his own people into the messianic banquet and casting the others into outer darkness. Luke carries the allegorization still further: the merchant becomes the king, and the whole parable an announcement and confirmation of the delay of the second coming.

The five *Parousia*-parables that we have discussed were originally a group of crisis-parables, intended to arouse a deluded people and its leaders to a realization of the terrible gravity of the moment. The catastrophe will come as unexpectedly as the nocturnal house-breaker, the bridegroom arriving at midnight, the master of the house returning late from the wedding-feast, the nobleman returning from his far journey. See that you are not caught unawares! It was the primitive Church which first gave the five parables a Christological meaning,[1] and regarded them as a warning, addressed to the community, not to become slack because of the delay in Christ's return.

### (b) *The Missionary Church*

The *parable of the Great Supper* has come down to us in a double tradition from Matthew and Luke respectively (Matt. 22.1–14; Luke 14.16–24). It is also in the Gospel of Thomas (64) in the version given on pp. 138f. A common feature of all three versions is the invited guests' refusal of the invitation and their replacement by anyone who could be found. We have here one of the numerous parables which, like those of the Labourers in the Vineyard and the Lost Sheep, already discussed, Jesus applied to his critics and opponents to

---

[1] Jesus only once explicitly designated himself in public as Messiah: Mark 14.62 par.

justify the good news when dealing with them: You, he says, are like the guests who slight the invitation; you would not accept it, so God has called the tax-collectors and sinners, and has offered them the salvation that you have spurned.

When we notice the divergences of the two versions, we find that in Matthew the parable has been strongly allegorized (see pp. 55–57f.), and that a second parable (22.11–13) and a generalizing conclusion (22.14) have been added. In Luke the parable serves as a story illustrating the warning in 14.12–14 to invite the poorest (see pp. 33f.); and it has been expanded to contain a second invitation to the un-invited (14.22f.). Let us look at this expansion first. After the servant has called in from the city's streets and alleys the poor, the maimed, the blind, and the lame (v. 21), there is still room in the dining-hall (v. 22). He is then ordered to summon more guests from 'the [country] highways and [vineyard] hedges' (v. 23); that is, he must go outside the city gates and call in the tramps as well as the city poor (v. 21). Since Matthew (22.9f.) and the Gospel of Thomas (64) refer to only one invitation to those previously uninvited, this repetition is an expansion of the parable. This development in the Lukan source may certainly be intended merely to emphasize the host's determination to have every place in the house filled. On the other hand, Luke may have read more into the double invitation. He may have understood the first invitation to the uninvited, which was confined to those in the city, to refer to the tax-collectors and sinners in Israel, and the invitation to those outside the city to refer to the Gentiles. For, as a comparison with Matt. 21.43 (the preceding parable) shows, Matthew probably understood the uninvited to refer to the Gentiles. But in Luke the doubling has given the picture more colour; he is particularly concerned to stress the introduction of the Gentiles into the Kingdom of God. As the Church was in a situation that demanded missionary activity, it interpreted the parable as a missionary command; the agreement of Matthew and Luke shows that this happened very early, but it could hardly have been the original meaning (see p. 51 above). This does not mean that the admission of the Gentiles to a share in the Kingdom of God lay outside Jesus' vision; but, as we can do no more than indicate here, he envisaged their participation in a different way, not in the form of the Christian mission, but as their coming *en masse* in the eschatological hour that was now imminent (Matt. 8.11f.). Here we conclude that the primitive Church interpreted and expanded this parable in accordance with its own missionary situation.

The Matthean version of the parable gives us a very similar observation. Its conclusion (22.11–13) has long troubled the expositors, as they found themselves confronted with the puzzling question why a man called in from the streets should be expected to have a wedding-garment. The favourite explanation that it was usual to provide invited guests with a wedding-garment (cf. II Kings 10.22) breaks down here, since there is no evidence of such a custom in Jesus' time.[1] On the contrary, the absence of the verses from Luke and from the Gospel of Thomas, as well as the striking change from 'servants' (vv. 3, 4, 6, 8, 10) to 'attendants' (v. 13), shows that vv. 11–13 are an expansion; and a comparison with an analogous rabbinical parable (p. 149) leads to the conclusion that the episode of the man without a wedding garment is a wholly independent parable; the beginning of this second parable may be found in 22.2, and may have caused the transformation of what was at first a parable about a private individual's supper (Luke 14.16) into one about a king (Matt. 22.2). Why did Matthew (or his source) insert the second parable? Clearly, care had to be taken to avoid a misunderstanding which might arise from the indiscriminate calling in of the uninvited (vv. 8ff.), namely, that the conduct of the men who were called was of no importance. Jesus was not afraid of this misunderstanding, as is shown by the other parables about the good news (see pp. 97–116)—e.g. the parable of the Prodigal Son; this will not

[1] The ceremonial garment mentioned on pp. 102f. is not an instance of a common custom, but denotes a special mark of honour.

be surprising if we remember that they were without exception addressed, as we shall see, to his opponents and critics.
But the misunderstanding was bound to arise as soon as
the parable was applied to the community, for v. 10 there-
upon became a saying about baptism: it opened the festal
hall to 'both bad and good'. But was not this saying about
baptism very unguarded and incomplete? In its missionary
activity the Church was continually confronted with the
danger that the gospel of the free grace of God might be
misinterpreted as freeing the baptized from their moral
responsibilities (Rom. 3.8; 6.1, 15; Jude 4). In order to
remove any ground for such a misunderstanding, the
parable of the Wedding Garment was inserted into the
parable of the Great Supper, introducing the principle of
merit, and emphasizing the need for repentance as the
condition of acquittal at the last judgment. Thus we see
again how the Church related the parable to its own actual
situation, and expanded it to meet a need arising out of its
missionary experience.

### (c) *Regulations for the Leadership of the Church*

In what has so far been said, we have repeatedly had
occasion to observe the process whereby parables that were
originally addressed to the religious leaders of Israel,[1] or to
Jesus' opponents,[2] were applied by editorial action to the
leaders of the Church. These transferences were suggested
by the symbols used (servant, shepherd), but also by the
need to find in Jesus' sayings some directions to the leaders
of the Church. The discourse in Matt. 18, which was com-
piled in view of this (see p. 30), shows how keenly the need
was felt. This factor also influenced the interpretation of
individual parables.

[1] See p. 43 (the Doorkeeper); pp. 44f. (the Servant entrusted with
Supervision); p. 48 (the Talents).
[2] See pp. 29f. (the Lost Sheep).

## 8 *Allegorizing*

In the previous section (pp. 36–53) we have seen that the primitive Church applied many parables to its own situation, which was characterized by the delay in Christ's return and by the Gentile mission. One of the expedients that the Church used in this reinterpretation was the allegorical method. In the forefront we find Christological allegorizing: the thief, the bridegroom, the master of the house, the merchant, the king, were all taken to represent Christ, where originally Christ's self-revelation was at any rate veiled, and only hinted at in a few of the parables. But also where reward and punishment were in question, there was, as we have seen, a readiness to seize on the allegorical interpretation (the supper of salvation: Matt. 25.21, 23; Luke 12.37b; the outer darkness: Matt. 22.13; 25.30). But the number of secondary interpretations is much greater. All the Synoptists agree in finding in the parables obscure sayings which are unintelligible to outsiders (Mark 4.10–12 and par. in their present setting). As the various layers of tradition differ in their use of allegorical interpretation, it will be better to deal separately with each of them. We shall begin by studying the material common to Matthew and Luke (*A*), and pass on to the Markan material (*B*), the special material of Matthew (*C*), the Gospel of John (*D*), the special material of Luke (*E*), and the Gospel of Thomas (*F*).

*A.* As far as the material common to Matthew and Luke is concerned, it has already been established that Matthew and Luke agree in applying the parables of the Burglar (Matt. 24.43; Luke 12.39f.; see pp. 37–39), of the Servant entrusted with Supervision (Matt. 24.45–51; Luke 12.41–46; see pp. 44f.), and of the Talents (Matt. 25.14–30; Luke 19.12–27; see pp. 45–49) to Christ and his second coming, in divergence from the parables' original meaning. The

agreement between Matthew and Luke in all three cases
justifies the conclusion that these allegorical interpretations
are not the work of the two evangelists, but belonged to the
tradition that already lay behind them.

The material common to Matthew and Luke supplies a
further example of allegorical interpretation in the *parable
of the Great Supper* (Matt. 22.1–14; Luke 14.16–24; Gospel
of Thomas 64[1]). The Matthean form of this parable, as
compared with the Lukan and the version in the Gospel of
Thomas, besides the expansion (22.11–14) already discussed
on pp. 51–53., and several merely narrative variants,
shows a series of divergences which spring from the
allegorizing tendency. The fact that in Matthew the 'man'
(Luke 14.16; Gospel of Thomas 64) has become a 'king'
(Matt. 22.2), and that the 'banquet' (Gospel of Thomas) or
the 'great banquet' (Luke 14.16) has become a marriage-
feast for the king's son (Matt. 22.2), might perhaps be
explained by supposing that this was the introduction to the
second, inserted, parable (Matt. 22.11–13) dealing with a
marriage-feast arranged by a king. But this leaves much to
be explained. As is shown by vv. 6f., we cannot attribute to
mere embellishment the fact that the single servant of Luke
(14.17, 21, 22f.) and of the Gospel of Thomas is replaced by
a number of servants—of whom the first group delivers
the invitation (22.3), while the second (22.4) brings the
message that the feast is ready—nor the additional feature
that in Matthew (22.3b) the first group is already rejected.
These two verses (22.6, 7), except the words 'The king was
angry' (cf. Luke 14.21), are an expansion, since they are
missing from Luke and from the Gospel of Thomas, break
the original connection between vv. 5 and 8, and entirely
destroy the setting of the story. We are told, for instance, in
v. 6 that the servants in the second group were not only
rejected, but were quite undeservedly ill-treated, and even
killed, by some of the guests (whoever they were). Even more
surprising is the anticipatory description of the king's anger

[1] For the text of the Gospel of Thomas see p. 138f.

when, before the marriage-feast, already prepared, has been enjoyed, he sends out his bodyguard, has those murderers (who all live in one city) put to death, and 'their city' burnt (v. 7). Evidently v. 7, using an old folk-theme describing a punitive expedition, refers to the destruction of Jerusalem, from which we are to infer that Matthew intends to represent by the first group of servants (v. 3) the prophets and the rejection of their message, and by the second group (v. 4) the apostles and missionaries sent to Israel (i.e. Jerusalem) and the sufferings and martyrdom (v. 6) undergone by some of them; the sending out into the streets (vv. 9f.) indicates the Gentile mission (see p. 51); the entry into the wedding-hall (v. 10b) is baptism (see p. 53). The feast to which the prophets bring the invitation, whose preparedness is heralded by the apostles, which is spurned by the invited guests and attended by the uninvited, and which may be enjoyed only by those who are clothed in a wedding-garment, is the feast of salvation; the inspection of the guests (v. 11) is the last judgment; the 'outer darkness' (v. 13) is hell (cf. Matt. 8.12; 25.30). Thus, by his allegorical interpretation, Matthew has transformed the parable into an outline of the plan of redemption from the appearance of the prophets of the Old Covenant, embracing the fall of Jerusalem, up to the last judgment. This outline of the plan of redemption is intended to vindicate the transference of the mission to the Gentiles: Israel would have none of it.

Luke is more restrained in his use of allegory. In his version of the parable there are certainly some allegorical features, though they are not carried by any means to such length as in Matthew. It is clear, however, from the introduction in 14.15, and from the expression 'my banquet' in v. 24, that he too regarded the supper as the feast of salvation. Moreover, we have already seen (pp. 51f.) that for him the 'city' is Israel, and that the parable symbolizes the call to the Gentiles. But the question arises here whether Luke himself could have been responsible for these allegorical interpretations. At any rate, the allegorical representation of 'city' as Israel, and of the supper as the feast of salvation, is not his work, but, as is shown by the agreement with Matthew, is older than either. The story's earthly setting (see pp. 138–142) suggests that Jesus himself did not tell it as an allegory of the feast of salvation, but he may well have had this in mind, as well as Israel's rejection of the invitation.

*B*. We turn next to the Markan material, with regard to which it may first be recalled that we have already found a secondary application of the bridegroom in Mark 2.19b–20 (see p. 40 n. 1), and of the master of the house in Mark 13.33–37 (see pp. 41–43), to Christ. As the latter instance is also found in Luke (12.35–38) and Matthew (24.42)— although Luke, and probably Matthew as well, are following their own special tradition—we must infer that it comes from the tradition already underlying Mark.

A further example of allegorical interpretation is the *parable of the Wicked Husbandmen* (Mark 12.1–11; Matt. 21.33–44; Luke 20.9–18; Gospel of Thomas 65). This parable, linked as it is with the Song of the Vineyard in Isa. 5.1–7, shows an allegorical character that is unique among Jesus' parables in the Synoptic Gospels. The vineyard is clearly Israel, the tenants are Israel's rulers and leaders, the owner of the vineyard is God, the messengers are the prophets, the son is Christ, the punishment of the husbandmen symbolizes the ruin of Israel, the 'nation' (Matt. 21.43) is the Gentile Church. The whole parable is apparently pure allegory. Yet a comparison of the texts shows that this impression can hardly be correct.

(1) With regard to the *introduction to the parable*, the description in Mark 12.1 and Matt. 21.33 of the careful construction of the vineyard agrees closely with the Song of the Vineyard in Isa. 5.1–7. The hedge, the wine-press, and the tower are derived from Isa. 5.1f. We can see at once from these early allusions to Scripture that the reference is not to an earthly owner and his vineyard, but to God and

Israel, and that we therefore have here an allegory. This
allusion to Isa. 5 is, however, omitted by Luke (20.9). More
significant is the fact that it is absent from the Gospel of
Thomas, where the beginning of the parable reads: 'A good
man had a vineyard. He gave it to husbandmen so that they
would work it and that he would receive its fruit from them.'
Still more significant is the fact that the Greek translation,
the Septuagint (LXX), has been used.[1] The connection with
Isa. 5 must therefore be due to editorial action.

(2) In the *sending of the servants* the secondary nature of
the allegorical features is even clearer. In the Gospel of
Thomas the introduction quoted above continues: 'He sent
his servant so that the husbandmen would give him the
fruit of the vineyard. They seized his servant, they beat him;
a little longer and they would have killed him. The servant
came and told it to his master. His master said: "Perhaps he
was unknown to them." He sent another servant; the
husbandmen beat him as well.' This description does not go
beyond the limits of a straightforward story; there is no
indication of a deeper allegorical meaning. It is specially
noticeable that in the Gospel of Thomas only one servant
is sent (both times). This feature also appears in Mark—at
least at first (12.2–5a)—although there the number of
sendings is increased to three. Three times a servant is sent;
the first is soundly beaten, the second is shamefully handled
with blows in the face, and the third is killed. Thus Mark
arranges the sequence of insults in an ascending order to
end in a climax; in arranging that order so that the third
servant should be killed, he is following a popular love of
climax which, in this case, is unfortunate, since, by anticipating the fate that the son was to suffer, he weakens the
course of the story. This feature has no allegorical significance. But by adding v. 5b the Markan form has abandoned
the popular triple formula, since there follows a summary

---

[1] The use of the LXX is seen most clearly in the phrase 'set a hedge
around it' (Mark 12.1); the Hebrew text of Isa. 5.2 has 'he dug it up',
which is replaced in the LXX by 'I fenced it round'.

account of a multitude of servants, of whom some are beaten and some killed. There is no doubt that this refers to the prophets and their fate. This allegory, obscuring the original picture, is certainly an expansion. It is characteristic of Luke (20.10–12) that he has not taken over the killing of the third servant, nor the allegorical conclusion of Mark. He has confined himself to the sending and ill-treatment of each servant, trimming the three incidents to perfect symmetry. We cannot now say whether his sober restraint is due merely to his sense of style, or to oral tradition. Matthew's treatment is wholly different (21.34–36). He has pursued the allegorizing method consistently to the end. The climax, as we find it in Mark, is completely spoilt. He starts by sending out a number of servants, some of whom are ill-treated, some killed, and some stoned. Then there follows only one more mission, more numerous than the first; its fate is the same. In these two missions Matthew sees the earlier and the later prophets; and the mention of stoning refers specially to the fate of the prophets (II Chron. 24.21; Heb. 11.37 cf. Matt. 23.37; Luke 13.34). Nothing remains of the original simple story as we read it in the Gospel of Thomas and in Luke, and may infer it from Mark—a story which only tells of a number of messengers going singly, each of them being dismissed empty-handed by the tenants and driven out with contumely and injury.

(3) With regard to the *sending of the son*, it must first be noticed that the actual story of his fate closes abruptly with his murder. That is also the case in the Gospel of Thomas, which continues as follows: 'Then the owner sent his son. He said: "Perhaps they will respect my son." Since those husbandmen knew that he was the heir of the vineyard, they seized him and killed him. Whoever has ears let him hear.' This conclusion, if nothing else, makes it impossible to see in the parable an allegory which the primitive Church would put into Jesus' mouth, since his resurrection had such a central importance for the primitive Church that it would certainly have been mentioned in the story. But in

the situation of Jesus, to which we are thus referred, we have to distinguish between what he himself meant and the way in which his hearers understood him. There can be no doubt that in the sending of the son Jesus had his own sending in mind, but for the mass of his hearers the messianic significance of the son could not be taken for granted, as it cannot be shown that the title 'Son of God' was applied to the Messiah in pre-Christian Palestinian Judaism. 'No Jew, hearing in our parable the story of the mission and the slaying of the "son", could have dreamed of applying it to the sending of the Messiah' (W. G. Kümmel). It is significant that in the rabbinical parable of the Wicked Tenants the son is interpreted as the patriarch Jacob (representing the people of Israel). That means that the Christological point of the parable would be hidden from the audience.

The primitive Church did not wait long to bring this point out. In the Markan form of the story, the son is killed inside the vineyard, and his body is then thrown outside (v. 8). This feature of the story simply emphasizes the full extent of the husbandmen's wickedness: they proceed to wreak on the corpse the final indignity of throwing it over the wall and denying to the murdered man so much as a grave; nothing here recalls the incidents of Jesus' passion. Things are different in Matthew (21.39) and Luke (20.15), who represent the son as being first thrown out of the vineyard, and then killed—a reference to the killing of Jesus outside the city (John 19.17; Heb. 13.12f.). Thus, in Matthew and Luke, the parable has a Christological colouring, whose first traces are, however, to be found in Mark: first in the words 'beloved son' (12.6), an echo of the voice from heaven in 1.11 and 9.7, and then in vv. 10–11, where in the form of the Old Testament symbol of the rejected stone which God (p. 11 n. 2) had made the key-stone (Ps. 118.22f.) there is introduced one of the primitive Church's favourite proof-texts for the resurrection and exaltation of the rejected Christ (cf. Acts 4.11; I Peter 2.7). This scriptural proof, which is a literal rendering of the LXX, was probably inserted when the parable was applied allegorically to Christ, because it was felt necessary to find scriptural grounds for the son's fate, and to add the missing mention of the resurrection. All these Christological interpretations are absent from the Gospel of Thomas.

(4) With regard to the *final question*, which is in all three Synoptists (Mark 12.9 par.), but is not in the Gospel of Thomas, it refers back again (see pp. 57f.) to Isa. 5.5, using not the Hebrew text (which is not in the form of a question) but the Greek translation. If the final question is secondary (the Gospel of Thomas has instead the call to hear; see p. 59), then so is the answer. Neither is part of the original parable.

But even if it is true to say that the connection of the beginning and the end of the parable with Isa. 5 is secondary, and that neither the sending of the three servants nor that of the son had originally any allegorical significance, yet the question arises whether the parable as a whole so far transcends the setting of everyday life, that it must have been intended as an allegory. Taking into account the amazing patience of the owner, the absurd expectation of the tenants that by killing the son they would obtain the title to the property (Mark 12.7), the killing of the son, one is bound to ask whether things really could happen like that. Strange as it may seem, the question can be answered in the affirmative. The parable is, in fact, a realistic description of the Galilean peasants' attitude towards the foreign landlords, an attitude that had been aroused by the Zealot movement whose headquarters were in Galilee. We must realize that not only the whole of the upper Jordan valley, and probably the north and north-west shores of the Lake of Gennesaret as well, but also a large part of the Galilean uplands, at that time had the character of latifundia, and were in the hands of foreign landlords.[1] It helps us to understand the parable if

[1] Thus, at the time of the First Revolt (AD 66) we hear of corn belonging to the imperial revenues, from the villages of upper Galilee, stored in Giscala; these villages, therefore, belonged to the imperial domains. At the same time Princess Berenice had stored large quantities of corn in Besara, on the boundaries of Ptolemais (Akko). At an earlier date, one of the Zeno papyri gives evidence of the fact that Apollonius,

we remember that the landlord is evidently living abroad
(Mark 12.1) and, indeed, is perhaps regarded as a foreigner.
The tenants can take such liberties with the messenger only
if their master is living abroad. In that case, he must, after
his messengers have been insulted and driven out, look
round for a messenger whom the tenants will respect. Thus,
if he is living in a distant foreign country, we have the
simplest explanation of the otherwise incredibly foolish
assumption of the tenants that, after the removal of the
sole heir,[1] they will be able to take unhindered possession of
the property (Mark 12.7); they evidently have in mind the
law that, in certain specified circumstances, an inheritance
might be regarded as ownerless property that could be
claimed by anyone,[2] with the proviso that the prior right
belonged to the claimant who occupied first.[3] The son's
arrival allows them to assume that the owner is dead, and
that the son has come to take possession of his inheritance.
If they kill him, they argue, the vineyard becomes ownerless
property which they can claim as they are first on the spot.
It may, indeed, be asked whether the killing of the son is not
too crude a feature for a story taken from real life. But to
produce the desired impression, the story had to intensify
the tenants' wickedness so much that no hearer could miss
it; their depravity had to be emphasized as strongly as

who was finance minister of the Ptolemaic kingdom from 261 to 246
BC, possessed a property in Baitianata in Galilee, from which wine was
sent to him in Egypt; the same place is mentioned in the Zeno papyri
as a commissariat station which supplied Egyptian officials with meal
on their journeys through the country. The latifundian character of a
large part of the Galilean hill country is explained by the fact that it
was originally royal territory.

[1] 'Beloved' (Mark 12.6) here implies 'only' (and therefore specially
beloved). He is thus the sole heir.

[2] Such a case arose, for example, when an inheritance was not
claimed within a specified period.

[3] A piece of land could be considered as lawfully taken possession of,
if no matter how small a part of it had been 'marked out, fenced, or
provided with an entrance'; we hear of a specific case in which a garden
that belonged to a proselyte who died without heirs was successfully
claimed by 'drawing a picture', i.e. by marking it with a sign.

possible. The introduction of the figure of the only son is the result, not of theological considerations, but of the inherent logic of the story. This does not exclude, but rather requires, that by the killing of the owner's son the parable may point to the actual situation, namely the rejection of God's definite and final message. Thus we are left with the conclusion that Mark 12.1ff. is not an allegory, but a parable referring to the existing state of things.

We can now answer the question about the parable's original meaning. Like so many other parables of Jesus, it sets out to justify the offer of the gospel to the poor. You, it says, you tenants of the vineyard and leaders of the people, you would not listen, but have opposed God again and again, and now you reject the last of his messengers. The cup is full. God's vineyard, therefore, will be given to 'others' (Mark 12.9). As neither Mark nor Luke indicates who the 'others' may be, we must follow the analogy of the related parables (pp. 100f.) and think of them as the poor (cf. Matt. 5.5).

We may sum up as follows: The mention of the vineyard is a potential allegorical element. 'The vineyard of the Lord of hosts is the house of Israel' (Isa. 5.7) is a verse with which the audience was familiar; and it implied that the tenants must represent Israel's leaders (Mark 12.12b; Luke 20.19b). The pre-Markan tradition took the allegorizing further by adding the interpretation of the servants as the prophets (Mark 12.5b); and by prophesying the resurrection it sharpened the Christological point of the parable (12.10f.). Matthew went a good deal further along the same road; in his version the parable (like that of the Great Supper; see pp. 55–57) became an exact outline of the story of redemption, from the covenant at Sinai, embracing the destruction of Jerusalem (21.41; cf. 22.7) and the founding of the Gentile Church (21.43), and passing on to the last judgment (21.44). Luke shows great reserve with regard to allegorizing, but does not entirely avoid it (20.13, 15, 17f.). The Gospel of Thomas is quite free from allegorical features.

Lastly, in connection with Markan material, we have to discuss the *interpretation of the parable of the Sower* in Mark 4.13–20 (the parallels in Matt. 13.18–23 and Luke 8.11–15 depend on Mark, as the context shows). For a long time I held out against the conclusion that this interpretation must be attributed to the primitive Church; but on linguistic grounds it is unavoidable.[1] To this we must add the important observation that the interpretation of the parable misses its eschatological point (see pp. 119f.); the emphasis has been transferred from the eschatological to the psychological aspect. In the interpretation the parable has become an exhortation to converts to examine themselves and test the sincerity of their conversion. These critical considerations are confirmed by the fact that the Gospel of Thomas leaves the parable (9) without interpretation.

We must conclude, then, that the interpretation of the parable of the Sower is a product of the primitive Church which regarded it as an allegory, and interpreted it in detail allegorically. First the seed is interpreted as the Word, and then, in a kind of table, the fourfold description of the field is interpreted as four classes of persons. This resulted from the fusion of two quite different conceptions, both of which are also met with in II (4) Esd.: on the one hand the comparison of the divine Word with God's seed,[2] and on the other hand the comparison of men with God's planting.[3]

All in all, it seems that, in view of the relatively small amount of parable material in Mark, the allegorical method

---

[1] For detailed evidence of this, see the complete edition, *The Parables of Jesus*, London and New York, 1963, pp. 77f.

[2] II (4) Esd. 9.31: 'I sow my law in you, and it shall bring forth fruit in you'; cf. 8.6. The comparison of divine commands with seed is unknown in the Old Testament. It has probably been formed under the influence of the Hellenistic conception of the *logos spermatikos* (cf. K. H. Rengstorf, *Das Evangelium nach Lukas*, Das Neue Testament Deutsch 3[10], Göttingen, 1965, on Luke 8.4–8).

[3] II (4) Esd. 8.41: 'For just as the farmer sows many seeds upon the ground and plants a multitude of seedlings, and yet not all that have been sown will come up in due season, and not all that were planted will take root; so also those who have been sown in the world will not all be saved.'

of interpretation had already gained considerable ground there. There can be no doubt that most of it belongs already to the tradition underlying this Gospel.

C. We now turn to our third layer of tradition, the special Matthean material. In the light of the preceding results, it will be no surprise, as we study its parabolic element,[1] to find far-reaching allegorical interpretation. We have already seen (pp. 39–41) that the parable of the Ten Maidens came to be interpreted—wrongly—as an allegory of the return of the heavenly Bridegroom, Christ. Similarly, at the end of the little parable of the Man without a Wedding-garment (Matt. 22.11–13; see pp. 51–53), which also belongs to the special Matthean material, we find a secondary allegorical interpretation, characteristic of Matthew and breaking the pattern of the story, in the casting of the intruder into 'outer darkness', where 'men will weep and gnash their teeth', i.e. hell.

The *parable of the Two Sons* (Matt. 21.28–32) receives in v. 32 a surprising application to the Baptist. He had had a similar experience to that of the householder in the parable —rejection by those who professed to be God's servants, and obedience from those whose way of life was ungodly. This application, however, is hardly original, for v. 32 does not fit in with the parable, as nothing is known of any change of mind in either of the two contrasted groups of people in relation to the Baptist. What is more important is that in Luke (7.29f.) v. 32 appears as an independent saying; the verse obviously became attached to Matt. 21.31 through catchword association ('tax-collectors and harlots'); more-over, the parable's original end[2] is seen in the formula (v. 31b) 'Truly, I say to you', which is more than once used at the end of a parable. Again we can see that a parable whose original purpose was to vindicate the good news (The

---

[1] 13.24–30 (with 36–43), 44, 45f., 47–50; 18.23–35; 20.1–15; 21.28–32; 22.11–14; 25.1–13, 31–46.
[2] Matt. 5.26; cf. Luke 14.24; 15.7, 10; 18.14.

despised people have accepted God's call, which you rejected; and so the promise is for them!) has in Matthew,
through its relation to the Baptist, acquired a soteriological
application which is utterly foreign to it, and is akin to the
soteriological interpretation of the parables of the Wicked
Husbandmen (p. 63) and the Great Supper (pp. 55ff.) But in
this case the application to the Baptist may well be the work,
not of Matthew, but of the earlier tradition; for, as Matthew
inserted the parable in his Gospel in connection with the
word 'John' (21.25/21.32), he probably found v. 32 already
there as its conclusion.

We now examine the interpretation of the *parable of the
Tares* (Matt. 13.36–43), which also belongs to the special
Matthean material and is of special importance for our
subject. This interpretation consists of two quite different
parts: in vv. 37–39 the seven most important categories in
the parable are interpreted one by one allegorically, giving us
a little 'lexicon' of allegorical interpretations; on the other
hand, vv. 40–43 are confined to interpreting the contrasted
fate of the tares and the wheat described in v. 30b, as the
destiny of the sinners and the righteous at the last judgment,
thus providing us with a little apocalypse. One is struck by
the fact that this interpretation contains a really unique
collection of Matthew's characteristic expressions.[1] In view
of this, we are forced to the conclusion that it is the work of
Matthew himself; and this is confirmed by the Gospel of
Thomas, which has kept the parable (57), but not the
allegorizing interpretation. The same conclusion holds
good for the interpretation of the *parable of the Seine-net*
(Matt. 13.49f.), which is simply a shortened reproduction of
13.40b–43.

We thus have in Matt. 13.36–43 and 49–50 two allegorical
interpretations of parables from Matthew's hand. These two
parables, whose first purpose was to impress on impatient
people the need for patience, insisting that the time for

[1] For detailed evidence of this, see the complete edition, *The Parables
of Jesus*, London and New York, 1963, pp. 81–84.

separation had not yet come, but that God would bring it in
his own time, was turned by Matthew to admonitory use
as an allegorical description of the last judgment, a warning
against false security.

These two interpretations bring out with special clearness
Matthew's pronounced tendency to allegorical interpretation. In view of the absence of any comparative material, we
cannot say how far the body of primitive tradition contributed to the allegorical element in his special material. But that
it did so is proved by the fact that both the application of the
parable of the Two Sons to the Baptist and his activity
(Matt. 21.32; see (pp. 65f.), and the interpretation of the
'others' as the Gentiles (Matt. 21.43) in the parable of the
Wicked Husbandmen are older than Matthew.

*D.* Before we turn to Luke and the Gospel of Thomas, it
will be well, for the sake of comprehensiveness, to look at
the Gospel of John. In the Fourth Gospel we meet with two
parables: that of the Good Shepherd (10.1–18), and that of
the Vine and its Branches (15.1–10). The parable of the
Good Shepherd has exactly the same pattern as the three
synoptic parables to which a detailed interpretation has
been attached, namely the Sower (Mark 4.1–9, 14–20 par.),
the Tares among the Wheat (Matt. 13.24–30, 36–43), and
the Seine-net (Matt. 13.47–50); sharply distinguished from
the parable (John 10.1–6) there follows a much more
extensive allegorical interpretation (vv. 7–18). On the other
hand, the metaphor of the vine and its branches at once
introduces an allegorical interpretation ('I am the true vine,
and my Father is the vine-dresser'), which has completely
absorbed the interpreted parable or metaphor into itself.
From this it can be seen how great a prominence the
Fourth Gospel has given to allegorical interpretation. But
John also uses metaphors that are not allegorical: 3.8 (the
wind); 8.35 (the slave and the son, where we should read
'for ever', and not [with Luther] 'eternally'); 11.9f. and 12.35f.
(the wanderer in the dark); 12.24 (the grain of wheat);

13.16 (slaves and messengers); 16.21 (the woman in travail). Closer to allegory are the metaphor of the bridegroom's friend (3.29), the group of sayings about the harvest (4.35–38), and also the numerous figurative expressions that the hearers misunderstood (3.3; 4.32; 6.27; 7.33; 8.21, 32; 13.33; 14.4, etc.).

*E.* When we turn to Luke and his special material, we meet with a surprisingly different picture. It is true that in the parables that he has in common with Matthew and Mark, or only with Matthew, he gives a series of allegorical interpretations, though these are less extensive than in Mark, and still less so than in Matthew. As we have seen, he interprets allegorically the parables of the Sower (Luke 8.11–15, pp. 64f.), of the Servants whom their Master finds waiting and serves (12.35–38, pp. 41–43), of the Burglar (12.39f., p. 38), of the Servant entrusted with Supervision (12.41–46, pp. 44f.), of the Great Supper, with its double invitation to uninvited guests (14.16–24, pp. 50–52, 55f.), of the Talents (19.11–27, pp. 45–49), and of the Wicked Husbandmen (20.9–18, pp. 57–63). But these allegorizations are probably without exception the work, not of Luke, but of the tradition behind him, since they are almost all to be found in the other Synoptists. Moreover, the allegorizing expressions and verses contain very few of Luke's linguistic peculiarities. But above all, the Lukan special material in its rich collection of parables[1] shows, as far as I can see, no examples of allegorical interpretation. On the contrary, the special parabolic material in Luke, in so far as it has been worked over, has been expanded and interpreted with a different purpose, namely a direct hortatory application. Luke has thus taken over allegorical interpretations from an earlier tradition, but has not himself worked over his material with this end in view.

[1] Luke 7.41–43; 10.30–37; 11.5–8; 12.16–21; 13.6–9; 14.28–32; 15.8–10, 11–32; 16.1–8, 19–31; 17.7–10; 18.1–8, 9–14.

*F.* If we finally look at the form in which the synoptic
parables have been preserved in the Gospel of Thomas, we
see that there are allegorical features only in the first of the
two versions of the parable of the Burglar (21b). 'Therefore
I say: If the lord of the house knows that the thief is coming,
he will stay awake before he comes and will not let him
dig through into his house of his kingdom to carry away his
goods. You then must watch for the world.' Here the expressions 'of his kingdom' and 'for the world' are allegorical
interpretations. Except for these two additions, the parable
of the Burglar, too, is free from allegory. The absence of
allegorical features from the Gospel of Thomas is very
surprising, because the gnostic editor (or compiler) of the
collection of sayings certainly understood the parables in an
allegorical sense, and intended them to be so understood.
This is clear, for instance, from the admonition 'He who
has ears to hear, let him hear', five times attached editorially
to a parable, with the object of appealing to the reader to
grasp these parables' secret meaning.[1] Thus, for example, the
Gnostics would have understood the pearl in the parable of
the Pearl (76) as a metaphor for *gnosis*, 'knowledge', just as
they understood the 'goods' that the burglar tried to steal in
the parable of the Burglar (21b). As the parables' wording
was not recast allegorically (except for the two additions to
the parable of the Burglar), but remained intact, the parabolic tradition preserved in the Gospel of Thomas is of
great value, for we discover them to be just as free from
allegorization as is the special material of Luke.

So we arrive at a strange result: the discourse-material in
Matthew and Luke, the Markan material, the special
Matthean material, the gospel as we have it in Matthew,
Mark, Luke, and John, all contain allegorical interpreta-
tions, but the Lukan special material and the Gospel of
Thomas have none. From the fact that the allegorical inter-

[1] Cf. the prologue and saying 1 of the Gospel of Thomas: 'These
are the secret words which the living Jesus spoke. . . . Whoever finds the
interpretation of these words will not taste death.'

pretations have been shown to be almost entirely secondary, it is fair to conclude that the whole of the parabolic material was originally as free from allegorizing interpretations as were the Lukan special material and the Gospel of Thomas. In his preaching Jesus confined himself to the metaphors then current, taken almost exclusively from the Old Testament: God = father, king, judge, householder, owner of a vineyard, host; in relation to him, men = children, servants, debtors, guests; God's people = vineyard, flock; good/evil = white/black (cf. Matt. 25.32); the last judgment = harvest; hell = fire, darkness; salvation = marriage-feast and great supper; the saved community =wedding-guests; and so on. He used these metaphors freely in his preaching, and on occasion added new ones—e.g., the end of the world = the second flood.[1] We can notice repeatedly how he makes such a comparison the starting-point of a parable.

How early the allegorical interpretation of isolated features of the parables began is indicated by the fact that, as we have seen from the study of the discourse-material in Matthew and Luke, the Markan material, and the special material of Matthew, it preceded the Synoptic Gospels; it evidently originated in Palestine. Of the evangelists, Matthew is the most addicted to its use; in Matt. 13.37–39 he actually provides a 'lexicon' of allegorical interpretations with seven items (see p. 66). The most reserved is the Gospel of Thomas.

Side by side with the desire to reach a deeper meaning, the hortatory motive plays the largest part. There is clear evidence of this in the reinterpretation of the parables of the Sower as an exhortation to the converted to examine themselves, in the crisis-parables' reference to the delay of Christ's return, and in the application of the parable of the Unjust Steward as an exhortation to the right use of wealth. Moreover, the soteriological interpretation that we find in Matt. 21.28ff., 33ff., and 22.2ff. may well have been

[1] Matt. 24.37–39 (Luke 17.26f.); Matt. 7.24–27 (Luke 6.47–49). But see earlier Isa. 28.15.

intended to serve the purposes of hortatory preaching; the instruction to the messenger in Luke 14.22f. would aim at intensifying missionary zeal. We have already mentioned (p. 9) the influence of Hellenistic allegory which would operate as a further motive in Hellenistic circles.

The result of this section of our study is that most of the allegorical traits that figure so prominently in the parables' present form are not original. That means that we must discard these secondary interpretations and features if we are to understand what Jesus' parables originally meant.


# 9 Collection and Fusion of Parables

## (a) *Double Parables*

We begin by observing that we find in the first three Gospels a great number of paired parables and similes where the same ideas are expressed in different symbols.[1] We find associated: patches and wine-skins (Mark 2.21f.; Matt. 9.16f.; Luke 5.36–38; Gospel of Thomas 47b in inverted order); a divided kingdom and a divided family (Mark 3.24f.; Matt. 12.25); lamp and measure (Mark 4.21–25; see p. 72); salt and light (Matt. 5.13–14a); a city set on a hill and a lamp (Matt. 5.14b–16; Gospel of Thomas 32, 33b, though here separated by a saying about preaching from the housetops); birds and flowers (Matt. 6.26–30; Luke 12.24–28); dogs and swine (Matt. 7.6; Gospel of Thomas 93); stone and serpent (Matt. 7.9f.; cf. Luke 11.11f.); grapes and figs (Matt. 7.16; Luke 6.44; Gospel of Thomas 45a); foxes and birds (Matt. 8.20; Luke 9.58;

---

[1] What is essential is the difference in symbols. Matt. 7.24–27 par. Luke 6.47–49 (house built on rock and sand), Matt. 7.13f. (broad and narrow gate), Matt. 7.16–18 par. Luke 6.43f. (good and bad tree), Matt. 12.35 par. Luke 6.45 (good and evil treasure), Matt. 24.45–51 par. Luke 12.42–46 (faithfulness and unfaithfulness of the servant) are therefore not double parables, but single parables arranged in the form of antithetic parallelism, and therefore not belonging here.

Gospel of Thomas 86); serpents and doves (Matt. 10.16; Gospel of Thomas 39b); disciple and slave (Matt. 10.24f.); boys and girls (Matt. 11.17; Luke 7.32; see pp. 127f.); two kinds of tree and two kinds of treasure (Matt. 12.33–35; Luke 6.43–45); the tares among the wheat and the seine-net (Matt. 13.24–30, 47f.); mustard-seed and leaven (Matt. 13.31–33; Luke 13.18–21);[1] the treasure and the pearl (Matt. 13.44–46); lightning and vulture (Matt. 24.27f.); burglar and suddenly returning householder (Matt. 24.43–51; Luke 12.39–46); tower-builder and king (Luke 14.28–32); the lost sheep and the lost coin (Luke 15.4–10); slave and messenger (John 13.16); prophet and physician (Gospel of Thomas 31). Whether in these cases the doubling is original is a question that must be examined for each case individually.

In the two parables of the Treasure in the Field and the Pearl (Matt. 13.44–46) the change of tense raises the question whether they originally belonged together; in fact, the Gospel of Thomas gives them both, but separated (the Treasure in the Field, 109; the Pearl, 76). This is not an isolated case; on the contrary, there is evidence that most of the double parables and double metaphors enumerated above were either transmitted alone without the other member of the pair, or separated from it by other material. The following have been preserved independently: the lamp (Luke 11.33); the measure (Matt. 7.2; Luke 6.38); salt (Mark 9.50; Luke 14.37); the disciple (Luke 6.40); the two kinds of tree (Matt. 7.17f.); the two kinds of treasure (Gospel of Thomas 45b); the tares among the wheat (Gospel of Thomas 57); the mustard-seed (Mark 4.30–32; Gospel of Thomas 20); the leaven (Gospel of Thomas 96); the treasure (Gospel of Thomas 109); the pearl (Gospel of Thomas 76); lightning (Luke 17.24); vultures (Luke 17.37); the burglar (Gospel of Thomas 21b; 103); the lost sheep (Matt. 18.12–14; Gospel of Thomas 107); the prophet (Luke 4.24). It would, however, be over-hasty to regard the

[1] Cf. Rom. 11.16: dough and twig.

pairing in all these cases as secondary; the falling out of one member of a pair may have taken place in an earlier strand of the tradition. There is, for instance, no reason to divorce the two parables of the Lost Sheep and the Lost Coin (Luke 15.4–10), although the first of these has also been preserved independently.

The only similes and parables that have exclusively been transmitted as pairs are: the patch and the wineskin; kingdom and family; birds and flowers; dogs and swine; stone and serpent; grapes and figs; foxes and birds; serpents and doves; tower-builder and king; slave and messenger.

From this collection it will appear that Jesus himself favoured the reduplication of *similes* as a means of illustration, choosing his pairs of related ideas preferably from nature, especially from the animal world. On the other hand, there is only a single pair of *parables* in our collection: the tower-builder and the king. In view of this fact, however familiar the twin parables may be to us, we have to examine every case to see whether they were originally meant to express the same idea. And even when this question can be answered in the affirmative, as in the two parables of the Lost Sheep and the Lost Coin, we must at least, in view of the general picture, reckon with the possibility that the double parables were spoken independently on different occasions, and not joined till later.

### (b) *Collections of Parables*

The primitive Church had begun early to make collections of parables. In Mark we find, besides the parable-chapter 4.1–34, a group of three eschatological[1] metaphors in 2.18–22 (wedding, garment, wine). In his parable-chapter 13 Matthew has brought together seven parables: he has taken over from Mark the parable of the Sower with its interpretation (vv. 1–23) and added to it a group of three parables introduced by 'another parable' (vv. 24–33), and then another group of three introduced by '(again) . . . is

[1] See pp. 91f.

like' (vv. 44–48).[1] Besides that, he has the following collections: ch. 18 with two parables about brotherly duties; chs. 21. 28–22.14 with three parables of warning; chs. 24.32–25.46 containing seven *Parousia*-parables. In Luke we have ch. 6.39–49 with a group of parables forming the third part of the discourse on the plain; ch. 12.35–59 with a series of *Parousia*-parables; ch. 14.7–24 with two supper-parables; ch. 15 with three parables about what has been lost; ch. 16 with two parables about the right and the wrong use of wealth; ch. 18.1–14 with two parables about the right way to pray: prayer should be persistent and humble.

We may pause for a moment over the last-mentioned example to remark that neither 18.9–14 nor, probably, 18.1–8 is really intended as an instruction about the right way to pray; both parables seem rather intended to show to Jesus' hearers God's pity for the despised and oppressed (see below pp. 111ff., 122ff.). So in trying to discover the parables' meaning, we shall do well not to be guided too readily by the meaning of the adjacent parables. How careful we have to be in this respect appears from the fact that all the seven parables, except the last, which have been brought together in Matt. 13, recur in the Gospel of Thomas, but independently and spread over the whole book (9, 57, 20, 96, 109, 76).

(c) *Fusion of Parables*

The tendency of the tradition to form collections of parables occasionally led to the fusion of two parables into one, the clearest example being the Matthean form of the parable of the Great Supper (22.1–14). We have already seen (p. 51) that in this case two originally separate parables about a marriage feast (the parable about the invitation extended to the uninvited guests 22.1–10, and the one about the guest without a wedding-garment 22.11–13) have been linked together as a pair of parables, and then,

[1] At the end of each group Matthew has added an interpretation (vv. 36–43, 49f.).

through the omission of the introduction to the second parable, have been fused into a single one. A second example is to be found in the similes of the two kinds of tree and two kinds of treasure. The simile of the two kinds of tree, which Matthew uses twice, occurs in the Sermon on the Mount (Matt. 7.17f.; 12.33) as an independent simile, expanded by the saying about the cutting down of the tree (7.19 = 3.10). It has then been linked to the simile of the two kinds of treasure to form a double parable (Luke 6.43–45). Lastly, in Matt. 12.33–37, by the insertion of v. 34, the two similes have been fused into a unity in such a way as to make the simile of the two kinds of treasure lose its independence, and to turn it into an interpretation of the simile of the two kinds of tree. A last example occurs in Luke 11.33–36, where the originally independent metaphor (cf. Matt. 6.22f.) of the eye as the light of the body (vv. 34–36) seems to have become an interpretation of the metaphor of the lamp (v. 33).

Sometimes parables are fused in such a way that only one or more features are transferred from one to another. We find, for instance, in the Markan form of the parable of the Doorkeeper (13.33–37) two features from another parable: the master's journey to a far country (13.34) comes from the parable of the Talents, and the handing over of authority to the servants (13.34) comes from the parable of the Servant entrusted with Supervision (see p. 44 above). Moreover, in the Lukan form of the same parable (12.35–38) the feature of the master waiting on the watchful servants at table (12.37) is derived from the simile of the serving Saviour (Luke 22.27), or perhaps from the symbolic action in John 13.1ff. Finally, in the Gospel of Thomas the parable of the Watching Servants (cf. Luke 12.35–38) has been interwoven with the parable of the Burglar. The second version (103) of the latter says, 'Jesus said, "Blessed is the man [cf. Luke 12.37] who knows in which part [sc. of the night, cf. Luke 12.38] the robbers will come in, so that he will rise and collect his [. . .] and gird up his loins [cf. Luke 12.35] before they come in." ' It is surely no accident that the two parables, thus interwoven, appear side by side in Luke (12.35–40). It is only a conjecture, though a well-founded one, that the form assumed by the parable of the Talents in Luke (19.12–27), differing so widely from the Matthean form, may be the result of a fusion with a second parable (see p. 46 above); this will have dealt with a claimant to the throne, who, after his claim has been recognized, returns as king, and metes out rewards to his friends and punishment to his enemies.

In one case we can actually watch the process by which a new parable has arisen from the fusion of the end of a parable with certain similes. This is in Luke 13.24–30, a passage which, as 'there' in v. 28 shows, is intended to be taken as a unity. Jesus is urging men to strive to enter by the narrow door (v. 24), before the master of the house rises (from his couch) and shuts it (v. 25a). He rejects the late-comers, since he will have nothing to do with the wicked (vv. 25b–27). Shut out, they can only wail and gnash their teeth as they see the patriarchs and prophets sitting at the feast of salvation, and the Gentiles at table with them (vv. 28f.). The interpretative conclusion is in the saying about the last who become first, and the first who become last (v. 30). A glance at the Matthean parallels shows that we have to do with a mosaic: through the fusion of the end of one parable (Matt. 25.10–12) with three similes that are related to it in illustrative content (Matt. 7.13f., 22f.; 8.11f.), a new parable has come into existence —the parable of the Closed Door.

If the attempt to discover the parables' original meaning is to succeed, we must discard all these secondary connections.

## 10 The Setting

We owe to the result of form-criticism the recognition of the fact that the gospel narrative's framework is largely secondary; and this is equally true of the parables. Synoptic comparison shows that the symbolic element has been transmitted with greater fidelity than the introduction, interpretation, and context. This is of great importance for a right understanding of the parables.

(a) *Secondary Context*

The parable of the Litigant on the Way to the Judge (Matt. 5.25f.; Luke 12.58f.) belongs, as we have seen (p. 32), to the crisis-parables. Its message is: 'Your situation is desperate! Come to terms with your brother before it is too late!' It is therefore one of the eschatological parables, looking towards an imminent catastrophe. In Matthew the emphasis is diverted from an eschatological to a hortatory purpose; there it serves, together with the simile of the offering (5.23f.), as an illustration of the need for reconciliation: 'Give way, or it may be the worse for you!' Thus in Matthew the parable has been inserted into an apparently appropriate secondary setting. The same process may be frequently observed.

In Luke, but not in Matthew, the parable of the Great Supper (Luke 14.16–24) is placed in the setting of table-sayings in which Jesus addresses, first, those invited (14.7), then the host (14.12), and finally one of the guests (14.15f.); it would seem appropriate to place a parable about a feast in a setting of table-sayings. Thus the parable in its present Lukan setting illustrates the advice to invite the poor, the lame, the halt, and the blind (14.12–14; cf. v. 21), whereas originally it was one of the numerous parables intended to vindicate the gospel message (see pp. 34, 138ff.). This was also the original purpose of the parable of the Lost Sheep (Matt. 18.12–14), which in its present Matthean setting illustrates the warning not to despise one of the little ones (see pp. 29ff., 105ff.). The parable of the Wicked Servant now illustrates the preceding exhortation to unlimited forgiveness (18.21f.), which can hardly have been its original purpose, since in the parable itself nothing is said about forgiveness. We shall deal later with the question whether Luke 11.5–8 is really an exhortation to unwearied prayer (cf. 11.9ff. and pp. 124–126ff.). All these examples, which might be multiplied, remind us that we must always examine critically the context in which a parable has reached us, so as to see whether it agrees with its original meaning in so far as we can recognize it. The question of its origins becomes specially urgent, as the Gospel of Thomas has transmitted all parables without any context.

### (b) *Secondary Situations and Transitions*

We must distinguish between the cases mentioned above, in which a parable has been inserted into an apparently appropriate context, and those in which, in the course of transmission, a situation has been provided for a parable or its interpretation. Thus we repeatedly find in the Gospel situations in which Jesus addresses a discourse to the public and later reveals the deeper meaning of his words to the trusted circle of his disciples: Mark 4. 1ff., 10ff.; 7.14f., 17ff.; 10.1ff., 10ff.; Matt. 13.24ff., 36ff.; John 6.22ff., 60ff. D. Daube has shown that we have to do here with a pattern that is to be found in rabbinical narratives from the first century AD onwards, and is especially used in controversies between Christians and Jews: a scholar is asked a polemical question by a Gentile or by sectaries, gives an answer, and when his interlocutor has gone, reveals to his disciples the problem's deeper meaning. But the probability that the above-mentioned passages imply this pattern, and are not drawing on historical reminiscence, is increased by the fact that the introductory verse of such instruction to the disciples often shows the evangelist's particular style, and also by the fact that we have already recognized as secondary the interpretations of the parable of the Sower (Mark 4.13ff.) and of the Tares (Matt. 13.36ff.), which are introduced in this way. In the Gospel of Thomas (20), too, a similar introduction to the parable of the Mustard Seed: 'The disciples said to Jesus, "Tell us what the Kingdom of Heaven is like" ', is secondary by comparison with Mark 4.30, where Jesus himself puts the question, since such questions from the disciples are characteristic of the Gospel of Thomas.

Moreover, the introductions to the parables themselves show an unusual number of the stylistic peculiarities of each evangelist; and we must therefore take into account the fact that much is due to editorial style. For example, it is no accident that in the parables of the Tares (Matt. 13.24–30), the Two Sons (21.28–32), and the Wedding Feast (22.1–14), which Matthew inserts into a Markan setting, it is precisely the introductions which betray the hand of Matthew. The situation in which each parable is set must therefore be tested to see whether it shows signs of editorial action.

(c) *Introductory Formulae*

The parables of Jesus, like contemporary parables, have two basic forms. We have (1) the parable beginning with a noun in the nominative (a simple narrative with no introductory formula): Mark 4.3 par.; 12.1 par.; Luke 7.41; 10.30; 12.16; 13.6; 14.16; 15.11; 16.1, 19; 18.2, 10; 19.12; Gospel of Thomas 9 (the Sower); 63 (the Rich Fool); 64 (the Great Supper); 65 (the Wicked Husbandmen); this is the form most commonly found in Luke; (2) the parable beginning with a dative (Aramaic *l*ᵉ). Most of the rabbinical parables begin with the words: 'a parable: like a . . .' This usage is an abbreviation of the following more detailed formula: '(I will tell you) a parable. (What shall the matter be compared with? It is the case with it as with) a . . .' So we find in the rabbinical parables a shortened form and an extended form of the initial dative.

In the parables of Jesus, corresponding to the introductory dative with a preceding question, we have in Mark 4.30f.: 'With what can we compare the Kingdom of God, or what parable shall we use for it? It is like . . .'; or in Luke 13.20f.: 'To what shall I compare the Kingdom of God? It is like . . .' Corresponding to the shortened form beginning with the dative we have 'like', 'as if', 'as when',[1] 'is like', 'may be compared to'.[2] The equivalent Aramaic *l*ᵉ underlies all

[1] Mark 4.26, 31; 13.34; Matt. 25.14.
[2] Matt. 7.24, 26; 13.24, 31, 33, 44, 45, 47, 52; 18.23; 20.1; 22.2; 25.1; Luke 6.45; 12.36.

these forms. This *l*ᵉ is, as we have seen, an abbreviation, and should not be translated 'It is like', but 'It is the case with . . . as with . . .' In many cases the content of the parable compels us to notice the shifting of the real point of comparison caused by this inexactness of the introductory formula. In Matt. 13.45, the Kingdom of God is, of course, not 'like a merchant', but like a pearl; in Matt. 25.1 it is not 'like ten maidens', but like a wedding; in 20.1 it is not 'like a householder', but like a distribution of wages; in 13.24 it is not 'like a man who sowed good seed', but like the harvest; in 18.23 it is not like an earthly king, but like a settlement of accounts. In all these cases we shall avoid error by remembering that behind the 'is like' there lies an Aramaic *l*ᵉ, which we must translate 'It is the case with . . . as with . . .' The same holds for the remaining instances in which the inexactness of the introductory formula is generally overlooked. After this, we should not translate the introductory formula of Matt. 13.31 by 'The Kingdom of Heaven is like a grain of mustard-seed', but by 'It is the case with the Kingdom of Heaven as with a grain of mustard seed', i.e., the Kingdom of Heaven is not compared to the grain of mustard-seed, but, as we shall see on pp. 116f., to the tall shrub in whose boughs the birds make their nests. In the same way, in Matt. 13.33 the Kingdom of Heaven is not 'like leaven', but like the prepared, risen dough (cf. Rom. 11.16), and in Matt. 13.47 the Kingdom of Heaven is not compared to a seine-net, but the situation at its coming is compared to the sorting-out of the fish caught in the seine-net. It may well be that this point is of great importance for the interpretation of the parables.

#### (d) *The Conclusion of the Parables*

What do the parables mean? What message have they for the community? What practical directions, what consolation, what promises, has the Lord given us in them? Such were the questions that occupied the mind of the primitive Church as it preached them and meditated on them. This helps us to understand why the most important expansions and recastings of the parables occur just where it is a question of the stories' meaning and application—i.e. at the end. The parables have come down to us with very varied endings, some being limited to the symbolic material, some inserting a brief comparison or a detailed interpretation, and some ending with an injunction, a question, or an instruction. In which of such cases is there an expansion? In trying to answer this question we shall do well to distinguish between expansions of the actual material of the parable and those that concern its application.

1. It is no accident, but rather agrees with what has been said above, that there has rarely been an expansion of the parable material itself, the so-called symbolic part. In some of these cases the cause of the expansion is purely external. To the little parable about the new wine which must not be put into old wine-skins (Luke 5.37f.) the tradition has added the sentence: 'And no one after drinking old wine desires new; for he says, "The old is good" ' (Luke 5.39; the Gospel of Thomas 47b with the sentence prefixed). The addition is unfortunate, for whereas the parable sets out the incompatibility of the new wine with the old (the new wine being the symbol of the New Age), the addition emphasizes the superiority of the old. The addition is obviously due to a purely external cause, the expression 'new wine'; it is a case of catchword association. A similar case, only not so obvious, occurs in Luke 12.42–46, in the parable of the Servant entrusted with Supervision. To this Luke has added a passage in antithetic parallelism setting out the different degrees of punishment inflicted on disobedient servants, according to whether they knew their lord's will or not (vv. 47–48a). The passage, which is not in Matthew, ill consorts with the content of the parable, as the latter is not concerned with knowledge or ignorance of the lord's will, but with the use or abuse of the entrusted authority. The description of the punishment of the unfaithful servant (12.46) has attracted to itself the saying dealing with the

varying degrees of punishment. See also, for the secondary
expansion of the end of a parable's symbolic part: Mark
2.19b–20 (see p. 40 n. 1); Mark 12.9 (see p. 22), again expanded in Matt. 21.41b; Matt. 22.11–13 (see p. 51); Luke
12.37b (see p. 41); Luke 19.27 (see pp. 46f.); finally, Matthew
has three times ended a parable with his characteristic
(Matt. six times, Luke once) closing formula 'There men
will weep and gnash their teeth' (22.13; 24.51c; 25.30); in
two cases he has prefixed to this closing formula the expression, also characteristic of him, 'into the outer darkness'
(found only in Matthew in the NT: 22.13 and 25.30).
Weeping and gnashing of teeth is there a symbol of despair,
always because salvation has been forfeited through one's
own fault.

2. Far more numerous than the expanded endings of the
symbolic part of a parable are the cases in which the expansion relates to the parable's application, either by
adding an application to a parable that has no interpretation, or by expanding an earlier application.

We shall first consider the cases in which parables without
an interpretation have been secondarily provided with an
application. Eight parables end abruptly with no explicit
application: Mark 4.26–29 (Patient Husbandman); 4.30–32
(Mustard-seed); Matt. 13.33 par. Luke 13.20f. (Leaven);
Matt. 13.44 (Treasure in the Field); 13.45f. (Pearl); 24.45–51
par. Luke 12.42–46 (Faithful and Unfaithful Servant); Luke
13.6–9 (Barren Fig-tree); 15.11–32 (the Father's Love).
Originally, the number of these parables in which Jesus left
his hearers to draw their own conclusions was considerably
greater; this can be seen from the Gospel of Thomas, where
all the parables except the Burglar (21b), the Great Supper
(64), and the Pearl (76) end without an interpretation. It is
easy to understand that a tendency soon arose to provide an
application for parables that had no interpretation. This is
most clearly seen in the three parables to which a detailed
interpretation has been secondarily supplied: Mark 4.13–20
(see p. 64); Matt. 13.36–43, 49f. (see pp. 66f.).

3. Very often an existing interpretation has been modified or expanded. The parable of the Unjust Steward provides a typical example of this; it may be recalled that in this case the old interpretation in Luke 16.8a has been enlarged by a whole series of further interpretations (16.8b–13; see pp. 35f.). In the parable of the Wicked Husbandmen (Mark 12.1–9 and parallels) three stages of the expansion may be observed: before Mark a secondary proof-text was added (vv. 10f.); Matthew and Luke have added to this an expository comment in the form of a description of the destructive activity of the stone mentioned in the passage from the Old Testament (Matt. 21.44; Luke 20.18), and Matthew has applied the parable to Israel and the Gentiles (Matt. 21.43); this constitutes the third stage, and disrupts the connection between the proof-text (v. 42) and its exposition (v. 44). Thus the three stages of the expansion are: (1) Mark 12.10f. — Matt. 21.42; (2) Matt. 21.44 par. Luke 20.18; (3) Matt. 21.43. In Matt. 21.32 we can recognize Jesus' interpretation of the parable in 21.31b as secondarily applied to the Baptist (21.32; see p. 66). The final command in Mark 13.37 is missing in Luke 12.35–38; Matthew has prefixed the same command ('Watch') to the parable of the Burglar (24.42); thus he (but not Luke) has enclosed the parable in two identical warnings. In the Gospel of Thomas, as against Matthew and Luke, the final command in the parable of the Burglar is expanded by the warning 'with loins girded' (21b). The parabolic saying about 'the sign of Jonah' is interpreted by Luke (11.30) as God's legitimation of his messenger through his deliverance from death; in Matt. 12.40 this interpretation is expanded and its emphasis shifted; the point of comparison is now the period of three days and three nights (Jonah 2.1). Specially noteworthy is the way in which the simile of the two kinds of tree acquires a new and secondary interpretation; it is fused with the simile of the two kinds of treasure in such a way as to make the latter an interpretation of the former (Matt. 12.33–35; see p. 75). The double simile of the city

on a hill and the lamp (Matt. 5.14b–15; Gospel of Thomas 32, 33b) is interpreted by Thomas, through the insertion of the saying about preaching from the housetops (33a), as referring to preaching; in Matthew it has two interpretations, one at the beginning (v. 14a) and one at the end (v. 16); the latter may have originally been an independent simile. An example of the way in which the meaning of an existing interpretation can be changed without a change in the wording is to be found in Matt. 18.35: 'So also my heavenly Father will do to every one of you, if you do not forgive your brother from your heart.' The words 'every one . . . your brother' originally have a quite general meaning: 'one another', 'everyone . . . the other', which is confirmed by Matt. 6.15 ('men') and Mark 11.25 ('any one'). Matthew, on the other hand, has limited the word 'brother' in 18.35 to the Christian brother, thus giving the parable a Christian application; for he makes 18.35 the conclusion of the great instruction to the leaders of the community in chapter 18.[1]

The warning cry 'He who has ears (to hear), let him hear' forms a special class of parable endings. In all three Synoptics it occurs only after the parable of the Patient Husbandman (Mark 4.9; Matt. 13.9; Luke 8.8), after the simile of the lamp, only in Mark (4.23), and after the simile of the salt, only in Luke (14.35); lastly, Matthew has it after the saying about Elijah (11.15), and as the conclusion of his interpretation of the parable of the Tares (13.43). On the other hand, the Gospel of Thomas gives the warning cry as the conclusion of no fewer than five parables, doubtless as an

[1] This limitation of the meaning of 'brother' is characteristic of Matthew. Following the well-established early Christian usage, he seems to use the word, except when it refers to a blood-brother, only of a Christian brother. This usage goes back to Jesus himself (Mark 3.33–35 par.). But if Matthew normally presupposes this meaning, it is clear that, as in Matt. 18.35, the limitation of the wider use of the word is generally due to a secondary Christian interpretation; thus Matt. 5.22, 23f.; 7.3–5; 18.15, 21; 25.40. It is probable that in all these passages 'brother' originally had the wider meaning of 'neighbour', 'compatriot'. This secondary Christianizing of 'brother' occurs in only two places in Luke (6.41f.; 17.3f.), and never in Mark.

appeal to the Gnostics to give careful heed to the secret meaning of the parables. This survey shows that the warning cry is in most cases secondary.

4. The most important result of the study of these secondary and expanded interpretations is that there was a strong tendency to add to the parables conclusions in the form of generalizing sayings. Where such generalizations are found, they are predominantly secondary in their present context; we must emphasize that what is secondary is their present place in the context, and that we are not in any way questioning the authenticity of the sayings themselves, but only insisting that they were not originally uttered as the conclusion of a parable. This is supported by the fact that they are entirely missing from the Gospel of Thomas. By using them in this way it was intended to give the parables the widest possible application. Typical examples of this tendency are that the parable of the Labourers in the Vineyard has been expanded twice in succession by a generalizing saying (Matt. 20.16a, 16b; see pp. 25f., 27f.), and that the secondary parable of the Closed Door (Luke 13.24–30; see p. 76) has been provided (v. 30) with a generalizing conclusion. The following parables and similes seem to have acquired a secondary generalizing conclusion—though this does not necessarily mean that the final verses are unauthentic:

The Lamp (Mark 4.22); the Measure (Mark 4.25); the Doorkeeper (Mark 13.37); the Labourers in the Vineyard (Matt. 20.16a, 16b); the Wicked Husbandmen (Matt. 21.44; Luke 20.18); the Wedding Feast (Matt. 22.14); the Ten Maidens (Matt. 25.13); the Talents or the Pounds (Matt. 25.29 par. Luke 19.26); the Friend who was asked for Help (Luke 11.10); the Rich Fool (Luke 12.21); the Servant entrusted with Supervision (Luke 12.48b); the Closed Door (Luke 13.30); the Unjust Steward (Luke 16.10, 13); Pharisee and Tax-collector (Luke 18.14b).

A survey of these generalizing conclusions shows that they deal only sporadically with guidance for daily life, and that most of them consist of eschatological promises, warnings, and admonitions. The realization that they have a secondary place in their context is of the greatest importance for the understanding of the parables concerned, because their emphasis, as a result of the new conclusion, has in nearly every case been shifted, often fundamentally. But even when the generalization agrees with the parable's meaning (Luke 18.14b), or at least is not incompatible with it (Luke 12.21), it is important to recognize its secondary nature, since, through the addition of such generalizations, the parables have acquired a moralizing sense which obscures the original situation and blunts the sense of conflict, the sharp edge of the eschatological warning, the sternness of the threat. The parable of the Labourers in the Vineyard, which is intended to vindicate, in an actual situation, the good news in the face of its critics, and to assert God's goodness, has been transformed, through a generalizing conclusion (the last will be first, and the first last), into a general instruction about degrees of importance in the Kingdom of Heaven, or about the unconditional nature of divine grace (see pp. 25–27). The parable of the Unjust Steward, which calls on hesitant people to decide on a fresh start in view of the threatening situation, has, by the insertion of the sentence 'He who is faithful in a very little is faithful also in much; and he who is dishonest in a very little is dishonest also in much' been transformed into a general moral lesson. Further, the recognition of these generalizing conclusions' secondary character is important for a complete understanding of the parables. It is in the addition of these generalizing conclusions that we hear the voice of the Christian preacher or teacher, bent on interpreting the Lord's message. They show us how early the tendency arose to make the parables serviceable in this way for the Christian community by giving them a general instructional or hortatory meaning. This is the tendency which finally transformed Jesus into a teacher of wisdom, and which, as we saw on pp. 12f., celebrated its greatest triumph at the close of the last century in Jülicher's exposition of the parables. This way of making it easy to use the parables for ecclesiastical exhortation was specially favoured by Luke (or at least by his sources), whereas Matthew sought to reach the same end through allegorical interpretation. So, if we are to recover the parables' original meaning, we must make up our minds to take account of this tendency and make allowance for it.

To summarize the results of our inquiry: The parables have a twofold historical setting. First, the original historical setting, not only of the parables, but of all Jesus' sayings, is their individual concrete situation in his earthly life. Secondly, they went on to live in the primitive Church. We know them only in the form that they received from the primitive Church, and so we are faced with the task of recovering their original form as far as we can. We shall be helped to do this if we observe the following laws of transformation:

1. The translation of the parables into Greek necessarily involved a change in their meaning.

2. For the same reason illustrative material is occasionally 'translated' too.

3. Pleasure in embellishing the parables can be noticed quite early.

4. Occasionally passages of Scripture and folk-story themes have influenced the shaping of the material.

5. Parables that were originally addressed to opponents or to the crowd have in many cases been applied by the primitive Church to the Christian community.

6. This often led to a shift of emphasis to the hortatory aspect, especially from the eschatological to the hortatory.

7. The primitive Church related the parables to its own actual situation, which was especially characterized by the missionary motive and the delay of Christ's return; it

interpreted and expanded them with these factors in view.

8. To an increasing degree the primitive Church interpreted the parables allegorically with a view to their hortatory use.

9. The primitive Church made collections of parables, which were sometimes fused.

10. The primitive Church provided the parables with a setting, and this often caused a change of meaning; in particular many parables, by the addition of generalizing conclusions, acquired a universally valid meaning.

The analysis of the parables with the help of these ten laws of transformation was, in the first five editions of this book, confined to the synoptic material. In the meantime the Gospel of Thomas has been discovered. The fact that this has confirmed the results of our analysis to a surprising degree shows that it was conducted on the right lines.

These ten laws of transformation are ten aids to the recovery of the original meaning of Jesus' parables. They will help us to lift in some measure here and there the veil, sometimes thin, sometimes almost impenetrable, that has descended on the parables. Our task is to return to the actual living voice of Jesus. How great is the gain if we succeed in rediscovering here and there behind the veil the face of the Son of man! To meet with him can alone give power to our preaching.

# III

## THE MESSAGE OF THE
## PARABLES OF JESUS

IF WE take into account the laws of transformation set
out at the end of Part II of this book, and with their help
try to recover the original meaning of Jesus' parables, we
find that the picture as a whole has been greatly simplified.
We find that many parables express one and the same idea
by means of varying symbols. Differences that are common-
places to us are now seen to be secondary. As a result, a few
simple essential ideas stand out with increased importance.
It becomes clear that Jesus was never tired of expressing
the central ideas of his message in constantly changing
images. The parables and similes fall naturally into groups,
and it may be suggested that ten groups emerge from our
study of them, and that these as a whole offer a comprehensive conception of his message.

## 1 Now Is the Day of Salvation

'The blind receive their sight,
the lame walk,
lepers are cleansed,
and the deaf hear,
the dead are raised up,
the poor have good news preached to them.'

This, according to Luke 7.22 and Matt. 11.5, is how
Jesus answered the question asked by the Baptist from

prison. It does not mean that all these miracles were performed before the messengers of the imprisoned Baptist so that they might relate to their master what they had themselves just witnessed (thus Luke 7.21f.); the main object of the passage is not to enumerate Jesus' miracles, but Jesus here takes up an ancient prophetic description of the messianic age (Isa. 35.5f.):

'Then the eyes of the blind shall be opened,
   and the ears of the deaf unstopped;
then shall the lame man leap like a hart,
   and the tongue of the dumb sing for joy.
For waters shall break forth in the wilderness,
   and streams in the desert. . . . .'

What Jesus says is simply a free quotation of this passage combined with Isa. 61.1 (the preaching of good tidings to the poor); the fact that mention of the lepers and the dead goes beyond Isa. 35.5f. implies that the fulfilment exceeds all hopes, expectations, and promises.[1] It is his cry of exultation: The hour is come; the blind see and the lame walk, and living water flows through the thirsty land—salvation is here, the curse has gone, paradise has come again, the end of the age is upon us, and manifests itself (as the Spirit usually does) in a twofold way, by deed and by word. Tell this to John, and then add 'Blessed is he who takes no offence at me' (Matt. 11.6; Luke 7.23). Blessed is he who believes, in spite of all appearances to the contrary.

There is another saying of Jesus closely related to this, taking up another passage from Isaiah (61.1f.): 'The Spirit of the Lord God is upon me, because the Lord has anointed me to preach good news to the poor. He has sent me to proclaim release to the captives and recovering of sight to the blind, to set at liberty those who are oppressed, to proclaim the acceptable year of the Lord' (Luke 4.18f.).[2]

---

[1] It should be noticed that Jesus omits the announcement of God's vengeance (Isa. 35.4).
[2] Jesus again omits the announcement of God's vengeance (Isa. 61.2).

The hour has come. Today this Scripture is fulfilled (Luke 4.21). The Creator Spirit whom the sins of the people had driven into exile with the last of the writing prophets now broods again over the thirsty land; the new creation has begun. The wretched hear the good news, the prison doors open, the oppressed breathe again the air of freedom, blind pilgrims see the light—the day of salvation is here.

'Realized eschatology' (C. H. Dodd) is also the meaning of Mark 2.19. To the question why his disciples do not fast, Jesus replies: 'Can the bridal guests mourn during the bridal celebrations?'[1] In the symbolic language of the East the wedding is the symbol of the day of salvation, as the language of Revelation bears witness: 'The marriage of the Lamb has come' (Rev. 19.7; cf. v. 9; 21.2, 9; 22.17). The day has come, the wedding songs resound. Here is no place for mourning. This is the time for the bridal festivities; why then should my disciples fast?

The sayings that follow, about the new garment and the new wine, may have been spoken on another occasion (Mark 2.21f. par. Matt. 9.16f.; Luke 5.36–38; Gospel of Thomas 47b); but in fact the three Synoptists have rightly connected them with the image of the wedding. They also describe foolish actions (using valuable new material to mend a tattered garment; pouring fermenting new wine into worn-out damaged wine-skins), and use traditional metaphors of the new age. There is no need to draw on the abundant material furnished by the history of religion where the cosmos is compared to the world-garment, in order to illustrate the symbols' meaning; we need only quote two New Testament examples. Heb. 1.10–12, following Ps. 102.26–28, describes how, on his return, Christ rolls the cosmos up like an old garment and unfolds the new cosmos. Even more significant is the passage in Acts 10.11ff.; 11.5ff., where Peter sees, in the symbol of the sheet tied at the four corners and containing every kind of living

[1] Mark 2.19 par. Matt. 9.15; Luke 5.34. The translation given above is established on p. 40 n. 1.

creature, the new cosmos restored and declared clean by
God. Tent, sheet, and garment are common symbols of
the cosmos. To this context Mark 2.21 belongs: the old
world's time has run out; it is compared to the old garment
that is no longer worth patching with new cloth; the new
age has arrived.[1] If this interpretation seems far-fetched,
the numerous examples may be recalled in which wine, the
subject of the parallel verse in Mark 2.22, is used as a
symbol of the time of salvation. For this, too, it will be
enough to quote a few biblical examples; extra-biblical
examples are legion. After the flood, Noah plants a vine in
the restored earth (Gen. 9.20). The deliverer binds his ass
to the vine, he washes his garment in wine, his eyes are
bright with wine (Gen. 49.11–12). The spies bring a bunch of
grapes from the promised land (Num. 13.23f.). In the story
of the miracle at Cana in Galilee in John 2.11, we are told
that Jesus manifested his glory, with the implication that
the wine is the symbol of the new age: in pouring out the
abundance of wine, Jesus reveals himself as the one who
brings the time of salvation. The old garment and the new
wine tell us that the old is past, and that the new age has
been ushered in.

The harvest, like the wedding and the wine, is a well-
established symbol of the new age. Harvest is the great time
of rejoicing:

'Thou hast multiplied the nation,
    thou hast increased its joy;
they rejoice before thee
    as with joy at the harvest,
    as men rejoice when they divide the spoil.' (Isa. 9.2).

'He that goes forth weeping,
    bearing the seed for sowing,
shall come home with shouts of joy,
    bringing his sheaves with him.' (Ps. 126.6).

[1] On putting on the new garment as a symbol of the new age, see
pp. 102f.

Harvest and vintage symbolize in particular the last judgment with which the new age begins. Joel (3.13) proclaims, in view of the judgment over all peoples, 'Put in the sickle, for the harvest is ripe. Go in, tread, for the wine press is full. The vats overflow, for their wickedness is great.' The Baptist depicts the coming one with the winnowing-fan in his hand, bringing in the harvest (Matt. 3.12; Luke 3.17). Paul, too, compares the last judgment to the harvest (Gal. 6.7f.). In the last book of the Bible (Rev. 14. 15) the angel calls to the Son of man, 'Put in your sickle, and reap, for the hour to reap has come, for the harvest of the earth is fully ripe.' And the angel with the firebrand replies (14.18), 'Put in your sickle, and gather the clusters of the vine of the earth, for its grapes are fully ripe'.

The hour has come, says Jesus, as he sends out his disciples, not to sow, but to reap. The fields are white (John 4.35); sowing and reaping go on together (4.36). 'The harvest is plentiful, but the labourers are few; pray therefore the Lord of the harvest to send out labourers into his harvest' (Matt. 9.37f.; Luke 10.2; Gospel of Thomas 73). The little *parable of the Fig-tree*, whose shoots and leaves herald the summer, is another saying concerned with harvest-time: 'As soon as its branch becomes tender and puts forth its leaves, you know that summer is near. So also, when you see these things taking place, you know that he is near, at the very gates' (Mark 13.28f. par. Matt. 24.32f.; Luke 21.29–31). Who is standing at the door? The Messiah.[1] And what is the sign that he is soon coming? In its present context, the answer is: the dreadful portents that herald the end. But it is doubtful whether this was the original meaning, since the present context (the discourse about the signs of the end) is a secondary composition, and the symbol of the fig-tree points in another direction: the fig-tree putting out its leaves is a sign of the coming blessing (Joel 2.22). Jesus intended the simile to direct his disciples' minds, not towards the horrors of the end of the age, but towards the signs of the time of salvation. The fig-tree is

[1] Luke 21.31, the Kingdom of God.

distinguished from the other trees of Palestine, such as the olive, the ilex, or the carob, by the fact that it casts its leaves, so that the bare, spiky twigs, which make it appear to be quite dead, make it possible to watch the return of the rising sap with special clearness. Its shoots, bursting with life out of death, a symbol of the great mystery of death and life, herald the summer. In like fashion, says Jesus, the Messiah has his harbingers. Consider the signs: the dead fig-tree is clothed with green, the young shoots sprout, winter is over at last, summer is at the threshold, those destined for salvation awake to new life (Matt. 11.5), the hour has come, the final fulfilment has begun, the Messiah is knocking at the door (Rev. 3.20).

It is the day of salvation because the Saviour is already here. The light is kindled.

Unfortunately we do not know what meaning Jesus gave to the *simile of the Lamp whose Place is on the Lamp-stand* (Mark 4.21; Matt. 5.15; Luke 8.16; 11.33; Gospel of Thomas 33b). According to the context, Mark and Thomas relate it to the gospel, Matthew relates it to the disciples (cf. 5.16), and Luke to the inner light (cf. 11.34–36). From the exegesis a conjecture may be hazarded as to what was the original application. What is the meaning of 'nor do men . . . put it under a bushel'? If a bushel-measure were placed over the small clay lamp, it would extinguish it. In the peasants' houses—small, one-roomed, and often with no window or chimney—this might well have been the ordinary method of putting out the lamp, for blowing it out might cause unpleasant smoke and smell, as well as a risk of fire through sparks. A free rendering, then, would be: 'They do not light a lamp in order to put it out again at once. No, its place is on the lamp-stand, so that it may give light to all the occupants' [all through the night, as is still usual among the Palestinian fellahin] (Matt. 5.15). The sharp contrast between kindling and extinguishing, which corresponds to the similar contrast between seasoning and casting away in the simile of the salt (Matt. 5.13), would be most intelligible if Jesus had been speaking with reference to his mission, possibly in circumstances in which he had been warned of danger and urged to protect himself (cf. Luke 13.31). But it was not for him to protect himself. The lamp has been lit, the light is shining, but not to be put out again! No, but in order to give light!

Jesus liked to speak of his mission in the various figures and symbols that traditionally depicted the deliverer. A thread of eschatological meaning runs through all the figures belonging to this category. The shepherd is sent to the unshepherded, oppressed flock, 'the lost sheep of the house of Israel' (Matt. 15.24; cf. 10.6; John 10.1-5); he seeks the lost sheep and bears it home (Luke 19.10); he gathers the little flock round him (Luke 12.32); he gives his life for the flock (Mark 14.27; John 10.11ff.); he will separate the sheep from the goats (Matt. 25.32), and after the great crisis he will again go before his own as their shepherd (Mark 14.28). The physician has come to the sick (Mark 2.17). The teacher instructs his scholars concerning the will of God (Matt. 10.24; Luke 6.40). The messenger calls people to the banquet of salvation (Mark 2.17). The householder gathers God's family round him (Matt. 10.25; Mark 3.35; Gospel of Thomas 99), and invites the guests to his table (Luke 22.29f.), and, as a servant, offers them food and drink (Luke 22.27). The fisherman appoints fishers of men in his service (Mark 1.17). The architect builds the temple of the new age (Mark 14.58; Matt. 16.18). The king makes his triumphal entry amid shouts of joy (Mark 11.1-10 par.), and the stones will raise accusing voices against those who would be silent (Luke 19.40). It should not be overlooked, however, that in all these metaphors the meaning is self-evident only to believers, while for the outsiders they keep the secret of the hidden Son of man still unrevealed.

God's gifts of salvation bear witness to the presence of the deliverer. Diseased bodies are restored to health, and death has lost its awful power, so that it is now only a sleep (Mark 5.39). The gospel is proclaimed, with its promise of the forgiveness of sins, the supreme gift of the messianic age:[1]

[1] J. Schniewind, *Das Evangelium nach Markus*, Das Neue Testament Deutsch 1[10], Göttingen, 1963, on Mark 2.12.

'God[1] forgives you your sins' (Mark 2.5). Among the manifold benefits of the new age depicted in the texts, one stands out with special prominence—the conquest of Satan. Jesus sees Satan cast down[2] 'like lightning' to earth from heaven (Luke 10.18); unclean spirits are forced to yield to the finger of God (11.20); those bound by Satan are set free (13.16). The strong man is bound, and his plunder is wrested from him (Mark 3.27 par. Matt. 12.29; Gospel of Thomas 35), since one has come who will despoil the strong of their prey, the Servant of the Lord, the conqueror. The binding of the strong man clearly refers to an actual experience, and therefore obviously to the temptation of Jesus. It seems, from an analysis of the accounts of the temptation (Mark 1.12f.; Matt. 4.1–11; Luke 4.1–13), that the three temptation episodes in Matthew and Luke originally existed separately, since Mark 1.12f. shows that the account of the temptation in the wilderness was originally transmitted separately; and the apocryphal Gospel of the Hebrews makes the same thing seem possible for the temptation on the mountain. It is better, therefore, to speak of three versions of the account of the temptation, rather than of three temptations. The subject (the wilderness, the gate of the temple, and the mountain) is the overcoming of the temptation to entertain a false messianic hope.[3] As this temptation has its *Sitz im Leben* in the period before Good Friday, and the political temptation did not exist for the primitive Church, we must not attribute the substance of the temptation-stories to the simple imagination of the primitive community. But in that case, in view of Luke 22.31f., where Jesus tells his disciples about a conflict with Satan, it may be supposed that underlying the different versions of the temptation-stories are words of Jesus in

[1] The passive in Mark 2.5 ('your sins are forgiven') is a circumlocution for the divine name. This fact is of considerable importance; see p. 11 n. 2.

[2] Cf. Rev. 12.9.

[3] J. Schniewind, *Das Evangelium nach Matthäus*, Das Neue Testament Deutsch 2[11], Göttingen, 1964, on Matt. 4.1–11.

which, in the form of a *mashal* (parable), he told his disciples
about his victory over the temptation to present himself as a
political messiah—perhaps in order to warn them against
a similar temptation. Thus we may conclude that the
different variants of the temptation-story should be closely
associated with Mark 3.27; by them, in the form of a
*mashal*, Jesus assures his disciples of the same experience
as that which in Mark 3.27 he asserts against his opponents
—now, at this very hour, Satan is conquered—Christ is
stronger than Satan.

When we examine the material, we observe that all the
sayings which announce that salvation is here are similes.
It is no accident that none of the elaborate parables belongs
to this category, but that, as the next section will show,
Jesus used them primarily as weapons of controversy, and
secondly to embody a threat or warning, and to illustrate
his instruction. Here, on the contrary, where his main
object was proclamation, we find him, in agreement with
the Old Testament prophets, especially Isaiah, preferring
terse similes.

## 2 God's Mercy for Sinners

We now come to a second group of parables—those that
contain the good news itself. The gospel in the true sense of
the word does not merely say that God's day of salvation
has dawned, that the new age is here, and that the Redeemer
has come; it also says that salvation is sent to the poor, and
that Jesus has come as a Saviour for sinners. The parables of
this group, which are the most familiar and the most important, have without exception one special characteristic
and one distinctive note which we shall recognize when we
see to whom they are addressed. The parables of the Lost
Sheep and the Lost Coin are addressed to the murmuring
scribes and Pharisees (Luke 15.2); the parable of the Two

Debtors is spoken to Simon the Pharisee (Luke 7.40); the saying about the sick is directed against Jesus' critics among the group of theologians belonging to the Pharisaic party (Mark 2.16); the parable of the Pharisee and the Tax-collector is likewise addressed to the Pharisees (Luke 18.9); the parable of the Two Sons is spoken to members of the Sanhedrin (Matt. 21.23). The parables whose subject is the gospel message in its narrower sense are, probably without exception, addressed, not to the poor, but to opponents. That is their distinctive note, their *Sitz im Leben;* their main object is not to present the gospel, but to defend and vindicate it; they are controversial weapons against its critics and foes who are indignant that Jesus should declare that God cares about sinners, and who are particularly offended by Jesus' practice of eating with the despised. At the same time the parables are intended to win the opponents over. How does Jesus vindicate the gospel against its critics? He does it in three ways.

1. First, in a series of parables, he directs his critics' attention to the poor to whom he is proclaiming the good news. The simile of the physician depicts their position vividly: Sick people need a physician (Mark 2.17). Do you not understand why I gather the despised into my company? Look at them! They are sick; they need help! The *parable of the Two Sons* (Matt. 21.28–31) goes even further with its closing words: 'Truly, I say to you, the tax-collectors and harlots go [at the last judgment] into the Kingdom of God before you.' The tax-collectors, for whom you regard penitence as almost impossible, are nearer to God than you are! For they may have disobeyed God's call, but they have shown sorrow and repentance. Therefore they, not you, are admitted into the Kingdom of God. But there is yet another reason why they are nearer to God than are the pious who do not understand Jesus' love for sinners, and this is set out in the little *parable of the Two Debtors* (Luke 7.41–43).

In order to understand Luke 7.41–43, certain exegetical remarks must be considered, from which the fact emerges that the episode related in vv. 36–50 has an antecedent which is not told. (1) The meal to which the Pharisee invited Jesus is clearly a banquet, as the guests are lying at table (v. 36);[1] it is in honour of Jesus, as Simon is allowing for the possibility that Jesus may be a prophet, which means that with him the departed Spirit of God has returned, bringing the new age. As it was a meritorious act to invite travelling teachers, especially if they had preached in the local synagogue, to a sabbath meal (cf., e.g., Mark 1.29–31), we may infer that before the episode related here took place, Jesus had preached a sermon that had impressed them all—the host, the guests, and the uninvited woman. (2) The designation of the woman as 'a sinner' (v. 37) indicates that she was either a prostitute or the wife of a man engaged in a dishonourable occupation (see p. 105). In view of v. 49, the former meaning is probable. Yet whatever she wants to convey through her tears, it is not stated. All that is disclosed is a boundless gratitude, since to kiss a person's knee or foot (v. 38) is a sign of the most heartfelt gratitude, such as a man might show to one who had saved his life.[2] How completely the woman was overcome by gratitude towards her Saviour is shown by the fact that unselfconsciously she took off her head-covering and unbound her hair in order to wipe his feet, although it was the greatest disgrace for a woman to unbind her hair in the presence of men; she was evidently so shocked at having bedewed Jesus with her tears, that she entirely forgot her surroundings. The fact that vv. 37f. describe a gesture of the profoundest gratitude (for pardon bestowed, as we see from vv. 41–43, 47) is confirmed by an important linguistic observation: Hebrew, Aramaic, and Syriac have no word for 'thank' and 'thankfulness'. This lack is supplied by the choice of a word that can imply the emotion of gratitude, e.g. 'to bless (in gratitude)'; in this case 'to love'. From this it follows that Jesus' question in v. 42 means: 'Which of them will feel the deeper thankfulness?' It also implies that Jesus interpreted the woman's actions as signs of gratitude (vv. 44–46), and

---

[1] The Greek text indicates this. At ordinary meals people were seated.

[2] We are told in the Talmud how a man accused of murder kissed the feet of the scribe to whom he owed his acquittal and deliverance from death.

lastly that in v. 47, too, the word 'loved' includes thankfulness. This shows conclusively that in the much-discussed passage in v. 47a forgiveness comes first (as, unequivocally, in v. 47b and in the parable), and it means that v. 47a should be interpreted as follows: 'Therefore I tell you that God [see p. 11 n. 2] has forgiven her sins, many as they are, because [= this can be seen by the fact that] she has shown such great thankfulness [thankful love]; one to whom God forgives little shows little thankfulness [thankful love].' The story therefore implies that Jesus in his sermon had offered forgiveness. It is against some such background that the parable of the Two Debtors must be understood. In it Jesus replied to Simon's unspoken criticism, and justified his having allowed a woman who was a sinner to touch him. Why did he allow this to happen?

He points out, quite simply, the contrast between the great debt and the small, the deep gratitude and the slight. Only those who have experienced the great debt know what goodness means: Do you not understand, Simon, that in spite of her sin-burdened life this woman is nearer to God than you are? Do you not realize that she has what you lack—a deep gratitude? And that the gratitude that she shows to me is directed towards God?

2. The critics of the good news have their attention directed, not only to the poor, but also to themselves. In the parables of this group the vindication of the gospel becomes a stern rebuke. You, says Jesus, are like the son who promised to obey his father's command, but afterwards ignored his promise (Matt. 21.28-31). You are like the husbandmen who refused year after year to give their lord his due share of the produce of his land, heaping outrage after outrage on him (Mark 12.1-9 par.; Gospel of Thomas 65).[1] You are like the respectable guests who rudely declined the invitation to the banquet—what right have you to pour scorn and ridicule on the wretched crowd that sit at my table? (Matt. 22.1-10; Luke 14.16-24; Gospel of Thomas 64; see pp. 138f.).

[1] On the text, see pp. 57-63.

3. But we have not yet spoken of the third line of attack, by far the most decisive, with which Jesus vindicates the proclamation of the good news to the despised and outcast. It appears most clearly in the *parable of the Prodigal Son*, which ought more correctly to be called the *parable of the Father's Love*[1] (Luke 15.11–32).[2]

The parable is not an allegory, but a story taken from life, as is shown by vv. 18, 21, where, in a periphrastic way, God is named: 'Father, I have sinned against heaven [i.e. God] and before you.' Thus the father is not God, but an earthly father; yet some of the expressions used are meant to reveal that in his love he is an image of God.[3] In v. 12 the younger son demands 'the share of property that falls to me'—that is, according to Deut. 21.17 (the firstborn gets twice as much as the other sons), a third of the property. The legal position was as follows: there were two ways in which property might pass from father to son—by a will, or by a gift during the father's lifetime. In the latter case, the rule was that the beneficiary obtained possession of the capital at once, but that he did not acquire the usufruct till after his father's death. That means: (a) In the case of a gift during the father's lifetime, the son obtains the right of possession (the land in question, for example, cannot be sold by the father), but (b) the son does not acquire the right to dispose of the property (if he sells it, the purchaser can take possession only on the father's death), and (c) he does not acquire the usufruct, which remains in his father's unrestricted possession till his death. This legal position is correctly reproduced when the elder brother is indicated as the sole owner (v. 31), while the father continues to enjoy the usufruct (vv. 22f., 29). In v. 12, however, the younger son demands not only the posesssion, but also the right of disposal; he wants a settlement because he proposes to lead an independent life.

[1] The father, not the returning son, is the central figure. Elsewhere, too, inaccurate and even misleading designations of Jesus' parables have sprung up (see p. 108 n. 1; p. 123 n. 1; p. 124 n. 1; p. 119 n. 2; p. 102).

[2] On this parable cf. J. Schniewind, *Das Gleichnis vom verlorenen Sohn*, Göttingen, 1940, reprinted in J. Schniewind, *Die Freude der Busse*, Kleine Vandenhoeck-Reihe 32, Göttingen, 1956, pp. 34–87.

[3] Cf. in vv. 18, 21 the solemn phrase 'before you,' in v. 20 '(he) had compassion', in v. 29 'command'.

Verse 13: After turning his property into cash, he emigrates. The size of the Diaspora, which has been estimated at over four million, as against a Jewish Palestinian population of half a million at the most, may give us some idea of the extent of emigration that was stimulated by the inducement of more favourable living conditions in the great mercantile cities in the Near East, as well as by the frequent occurrence of famine in Palestine. The fact that the younger son is evidently unmarried allows us to draw conclusions about his age: the normal marriageable age for a man was eighteen to twenty. Verse 15: He had to be in contact with unclean animals (Lev. 11.7), and could not observe the sabbath, so he was reduced to the lowest depths of degradation and practically forced to deny his religion at every turn.[1] Verse 16 raises the question why he did not eat any of the swine's food. The answer is supplied by translating the verse: 'And he would have been only too glad to fill his belly with the carob-beans with which the swine were fed [*sc.* but he was too disgusted to do so], and no one gave him [*sc.* anything to eat].' Therefore he had to steal what food he got. Verse 17: 'He came to himself' is in Hebrew and Aramaic an expression of repentance. Verse 18: 'And go to my father' = 'and go home'; an oriental would not think it suitable to mention the mother, but she is included here, as a matter of course, and also in what follows. Verse 19: 'Treat me as one of your hired servants': after the legal settlement he has no further claim, even to food and clothing; he will ask to be allowed to earn both. Verse 20: 'Ran'—a most unusual and undignified procedure for an aged oriental, even though he is in the greatest haste. 'Kissed him': the kiss is (as in II Sam. 14.33) a sign of forgiveness. Verse 21 = 18f., except for the final words 'treat . . . servants', which the father does not allow his son to utter; instead, he changes the unspoken words to their opposite, and treats the returning one, not as a wage-earner, but as an honoured guest.

In vv. 22f. the father gives three orders with which Gen. 41.42 may be compared: when Joseph was appointed chief vizier, he received from Pharaoh a ring, a robe of fine linen, and a golden chain: (1) First comes the ceremonial robe, which in the East is a mark of high distinction. There is no bestowal of orders, but when a king wants to honour a deserving official, he presents him

[1] 'Cursed be the man who breeds swine,' says the Talmud.

with a costly robe; investiture with a new garment is therefore a symbol of the new age. In other words, the son is treated as a guest of honour. (2) The ring and the shoes: excavations have shown that the ring is to be regarded as a signet-ring; the gift of a ring signified the bestowal of authority (cf. I Macc. 6.15). Shoes are a luxury, worn by free men; here they mean that the son is no longer to go about barefoot like a slave. (3) As a rule, meat is rarely eaten. For special occasions a fatted calf is prepared. Its killing means a feast for the family and the servants, and the festal reception of the returning son to the family table. The three orders given by the father are the manifest tokens of forgiveness and reinstatement, evident to all. In v. 24 we have two most vivid images in synonymous parallelism; both describe the change: resurrection from the dead, and the finding of the lost sheep. Verse 25: After the feast comes music (loud singing and hand-clapping) and dancing by the men. Verse 29: The elder son omits the address, and heaps reproaches on his father. Verse 30: He avoids giving the returned prodigal the name of brother; 'this' is here used contemptuously, as in Matt. 20.12; Luke 18.11; Acts 17.18. Verse 31: Unlike v. 29, the father's address is specially affectionate, 'my son' = 'my dear boy'.

The parable describes with the most impressive simplicity what God is like—his goodness, his grace, his great mercy, his abounding love. He rejoices over the return of the lost, like the father who prepared the feast of welcome. But this is only the content of the first half (vv. 11–24), for the parable has a double climax: it describes not only the return of the younger son, but also the protest of the elder brother; and the division is emphasized by the fact that each half of the parable ends with the same saying as a sort of refrain (vv. 24, 32). As the first half is complete in itself, the second half appears at first sight superfluous. But there is no reason whatever to regard the second part as an addition. Linguistically and factually it fits the pattern of the story, without allegorizing or distorting it; it has a foundation in v. 11, and the contrast between the two sons has an analogy in Matt. 21.28–31. Why did Jesus include it? There can be only one answer: because of the actual situation. The parable was addressed to men who were like the elder brother, men who were offended at the gospel. It was meant as an appeal to their conscience; Jesus says to them: See the greatness of God's love for his lost children, and contrast it with your own joyless, loveless, unthankful, and self-righteous lives. Cease from your loveless ways, and be merciful. The spiritually dead are rising to new life, the lost are returning home; rejoice with them. So we see that, as in the other three two-edged parables, the emphasis falls on the second half.[1] The parable of the Prodigal Son is therefore not primarily a proclamation of the good news to the poor, but a vindication of it in reply to its critics. Jesus' justification lies in the boundless love of God. But he does not remain on the defensive: the parable breaks off abruptly, and the issue is still open. No doubt this reflects the situation that confronted him. His hearers were in the position of the elder son who had to decide whether he would accept his father's invitation and share his joy. So Jesus does not pronounce sentence; he still has hopes, and he would help them to abandon their resistance to the gospel, to realize how their self-righteousness and lovelessness separate them from God, and to come to experience the great joy that the good news brings (v. 32a). The vindication of the good news takes the form of a reproach and an appeal to the hearts of its critics.

The recognition that Luke 15.11–32 is primarily an apologetic parable, in which Jesus justifies his table companionship with sinners against his critics (cf. vv. 1f.), carries with it a very important consequence. As we have seen, Jesus justifies his revolutionary conduct by claiming in the parable: God's love to the returning sinner knows no bounds. What I do represents God's nature and will. *Jesus thus claims that in his actions God's love to the repentant sinner is made effectual.* So the parable, without making any kind of Christological statement, reveals itself as a veiled

[1] On Matt. 20.1–15, see pp. 28f.; on 22.1–14, see pp. 51f.; on Luke 16.19–31, see p. 147.

assertion of authority: Jesus claims that he is acting in God's stead, that he is God's representative.

The twin *parables of the Lost Sheep* (Luke 15.4–7; Matt. 18.12–14) and *the Lost Coin* (Luke 15.8–10)[1] are closely related to the parable of the Prodigal Son.

In Luke 15.2 we are told that Jesus received tax-collectors and 'sinners' and ate with them. The term 'sinners' means: (1) people who led an immoral life (e.g., adulterers, swindlers: Luke 18.11), and (2) people who followed a dishonourable occupation (i.e. one that notoriously involved dishonesty or immorality), and who were on that account deprived of civil rights, such as holding office or bearing witness in legal proceedings—e.g. customs officers, tax-collectors, shepherds, donkey-drivers, pedlars, and tanners. When the Pharisees and scribes asked why Jesus accepted such people as table companions, they were not expressing surprise but disapproval; they were implying that he was an irreligious man, and inviting his followers to dissociate themselves from him. Verses 4–10: The twin parables, which contain Jesus' reply, play on the contrast between man and woman, and perhaps also between rich and poor. It is true that the owner of the flock was not a very rich man. Among the Bedouin the size of a flock varies from 20 to 200 head; in Jewish law 300 head is reckoned an unusually large flock. So the man with 100 sheep owns a medium-sized flock; he looks after it himself (like the man in John 10.11f.), as he cannot afford a watchman. Although he is no Croesus, he is well off in comparison with the poor widow.

In the Gospel of Thomas (107) the parable of the Lost Sheep reads as follows: 'Jesus said: The Kingdom is like a shepherd who has a hundred sheep. One of them—the largest—went astray. He left the ninety-nine, and sought for this one till he found it. Having tired himself out, he said to the sheep, "I love thee more than the ninety-nine".' In Luke the parable, as far as v. 6, is a question. Verse 4: 'What man of you': shepherds were reckoned among the 'sinners', because they were suspected of driving their flocks into foreign fields and of embezzling the proceeds; but that did not prevent Jesus from using the shepherd as an image of God's loving action. 'If he has lost one of them': A Palestinian

---

[1] On the parable of the Lost Sheep, see pp. 29–31.

shepherd counts his flock before putting them into the fold at
night, to make sure that none of the animals is lost. The number
ninety-nine implies that they have just been counted. 'Does not
leave the ninety-nine': Experts on Palestinian life agree that a
shepherd cannot possibly leave his flock to itself. If he has to
look for a lost animal, he leaves the others in charge of the shepherds who share the fold with him (Luke 2.8; John 10.4f.), or he
drives them into a cave. The young goatherd Muhammad ed-
Deeb, who discovered Qumran Cave 1, counted his flock at the
unusual hour of 11 a.m., because he had twice omitted to count
them in the evening; before he set off in search of his lost goat,
he asked two fellow goatherds with whom he was in the habit
of going out to look after his flock (55 head). 'In the wilderness'
means here the fold or the pasture-ground in the desolate
hill-country. 'And go after the one which is lost': In the Gospel
of Thomas the motive for the shepherd's laborious search
is the loss of the largest and most valuable beast, which he
loved more than all the rest; but this is a complete misunderstanding of the parable, as can be seen from a comparison with
Matthew and Luke, as well as with the general trend of Jesus'
message. For the expression in Matthew (v. 14), 'one of these little
ones', and the setting of the parable in Luke, with v. 5, suggest
that the lost sheep was probably thought of as a specially weak
one. It was not the animal's high value that caused the shepherd
to set out on his search, but simply the fact that it belonged to
him, and that without his help it could not find its way back
to the flock. The statement in v. 5 (not in Matthew) that the
shepherd 'lays it on his shoulders' when he has found it simply
describes a daily occurrence in the Near East. When a sheep has
strayed from the flock and roamed about, it usually lies down
dejectedly, and cannot be brought to stand up or run; so there is
nothing for the shepherd to do but to carry it, and over long
distances this can only be done by putting it on his shoulders,
i.e. round his neck; he grasps its fore- and hind-legs with each
hand, or if he needs one hand free for his shepherd's staff, he
holds all four legs firmly with one hand against his breast. Verse
6: 'He calls' (cf. v. 9) suggests the preparation of a feast (cf. v. 23).

Verse 8: In the parable of the Lost Coin, which, as far as v. 9,
is also to be read as a question, the ten drachmas will remind
everyone who is familiar with Arab Palestine of the woman's
head-dress, bedecked with coins, which is part of her dowry,

representing her most precious possession and her nest-egg, which may not be laid aside, even in sleep; in fact, it is mentioned in rabbinic literature that gold dinars are worn as ornaments. If the woman's ten drachmas were on her head-dress, they formed a very modest adornment, seeing that today in the East many a woman prides herself on a head-dress of hundreds of gold and silver coins. The woman 'lights a lamp', not because it is night, but because the low door lets very little light into the miserable, windowless (see p. 94) dwelling; and she 'sweeps the house' with a palm-twig, because in the dark the broom may make the coin tinkle on the stone floor. Verse 9: If 'she calls together' is to be understood here as a reference to preparing a feast, it could, in the case of the poor woman, be interpreted as merely a modest entertainment of her friends and neighbours.

Both parables end with a sentence that contains a paraphrase for the divine name, since emotions must not be ascribed to God. We must therefore translate Luke 15.7: 'Thus *God* [at the last judgment; see below] will rejoice more over one sinner who has repented than over ninety-nine respectable [righteous] persons who have not committed any gross sin[1]' (according to Matt. 18.14: 'So is *God* pleased when one of the least important escapes doom'); and correspondingly Luke 15.10 should be translated: 'Thus, I say to you, *God*[2] will rejoice over one sinner who has repented.' The point of comparison in Luke 15.4–7 is not the intimate bond between the shepherd and the flock (as in John 10, but this does not suit Luke 15.8–10), nor the unwearied search (as in Matt. 18.12–14 in the present context; see p. 30), but simply and solely the joy of finding what was lost. As the shepherd rejoices over the lamb brought home, and the poor woman over her recovered drachma, so will God rejoice. The future tense in Luke 15.7 is to be understood as referring to the last days: at the final judgment God will rejoice when among the many righteous

[1] This is the meaning of 'who need no repentance'.
[2] 'Before the angels of God' is a circumlocution for 'before God', and to speak of 'joy before God' is a reverential form of saying that 'he rejoices'.

he finds a sinner who has repented and on whom he may pronounce absolution—indeed, it will give him even greater joy. Such is God's character: he wants the lost to be redeemed, because they are his; their wanderings have grieved him, and he rejoices at their return home. It is God's 'redemptive joy', of which Jesus speaks—the joy of forgiving. This is Jesus' defence of the gospel: Because God's mercy is so infinite that his supreme joy is in forgiving, my mission as Saviour is to wrest Satan's prey from him and to bring home the lost. Once again—Jesus is God's representative (see p. 105).

As we have already seen on pp. 27–29, the *parable of the Good Employer* (Matt. 20.1–15) is also concerned with the justification of the gospel against its critics.[1]

Verse 1: We have a parable with a datival opening: 'Thus it is with the Kingdom of God' (see pp. 79f.). The Kingdom here is not compared to the master of the house, nor to the labourers or the vineyard, but, as so often, its arrival is compared to a reckoning.[2] In Matt. 20.1, therefore, as throughout Jesus' preaching, the Kingdom of God is to be understood in an eschatological sense. Verse 2: A denarius is the usual day's wage for a labourer. Verse 3: 'About the third hour' = between eight and nine a.m.[3] 'Standing idle in the market place': 'standing' here has the weakened sense of being present, as in John 1.26; 18.18; Matt. 13.2. No oriental stands for hours in the market place; they are therefore sitting about and gossiping idly. Verse 4: 'Whatever is right': they would understand by this that their pay would be a fraction of a denarius. Verse 6: The fact that between four and five p.m. the master of the house was still looking for more labour shows that the work was unusually urgent. The

[1] The employer is the central figure; the usual title ('The Labourers in the Vineyard') obscures that fact (cf. p. 101 n. 1).

[2] Matt. 25. 14ff. par. Luke 19.12ff.; Luke 16.2; cf. Matt. 6.2, 5, 16; 24.45ff. par. Luke 12.42ff.; Matt. 18.23ff.; see p. 164.

[3] Although the day began at sunset (cf. the 'hallowing' of the Sabbath on Friday evening), the hours of the day were reckoned from sunrise—naturally, because there were no clocks. The night, on the other hand, was not divided into hours, but into three (Luke 12.38) night-watches (cf. p. 19, especially n. 1).

vintage and the pressing had to be finished before the onset of
the rainy season with its cool nights; if there were a heavy yield,
the race against time would become serious. The question in v. 6b
does not express surprise, but reproach. Verse 7: The lame excuse is a cover for their characteristic oriental indifference. Verse
8: The payment of wages in the evening is such a matter of course
(Lev. 19.13; Deut. 24.14f.) that the issuing of a special order
suggests that the owner had some definite purpose in mind. This
special intention was certainly not, as it might seem at first, that
the last should be the first to receive their wages, but that all,
without exception, should receive the full day's wages. 'Pay
them their wages' therefore means 'pay the full day's wages',
and 'beginning' may have the weakened meaning of 'including'.
Verse 11: 'At the householder': the master of the house is hardly
likely to be present, and so they go with their noisy complaints
to his house. Verse 12: 'These last': the unduly privileged
labourers had no reason to take part in the action of their own
accord; so the complainants must have forced them to come with
them. In their indignation they omit the address (cf. Luke 15.29).
They have suffered a glaring double injustice: (1) they have been
obliged to work for twelve hours, as against the others' one hour;
and (2) they have had to work in the burning midday heat,
whereas the others worked in the cool of the evening. They
therefore consider that the duration and hardship of their work
entitle them to a much higher rate of pay. Verse 13: 'To one of
them': he picks out the chief objector. 'Friend': they had omitted
the address; the master of the house puts them to shame by his
mode of addressing them (cf. Luke 15.31; cf. p. 103). 'My
friend' is a way of addressing someone whose name one does
not know; here it is at once friendly and reproachful—'my dear
fellow'. In all three places in the New Testament where this
address occurs (Matt. 20.13; 22.12; 26.50), the person addressed
is in the wrong. Verse 15: 'With what belongs to me': the original
meaning is 'on my own estate'. On v. 16, see pp. 27f.

The clearness and simplicity with which this parable presents
the good news is thrown into sharp relief by comparison with a
rabbinical parallel that has been preserved in the Jerusalem
Talmud. A distinguished scholar, Rabbi Bun bar Chijja, died at
an early age *c.* AD 325, on the day on which his son and name-
sake, later known as Rabbi Bun II, was born. His former teachers,
who had become his colleagues, assembled to pay him the last

honours; and one of them, Rabbi Ze'era, pronounced his funeral oration, which he introduced with a parable. He began by saying that the situation was like that of a king who had hired a great number of labourers. Two hours after the work had begun, he inspected them, and saw that one of them was more skilful and industrious than the others. He took him by the hand and walked up and down with him till the evening. When the labourers came to receive their wages, this one received the same amount as the others. Then they grumbled and said, 'We have worked the whole day, against this man's two hours, and yet you have paid him the full day's wages'. The king replied, 'I have not wronged you; this labourer has done more in two hours than you have done in the whole day.' In the same way, concluded the funeral oration, Rabbi Bun bar Chijja has accomplished more in his short life of twenty-eight years than many a grey-haired scholar in a hundred years (*sc*. therefore, after so brief a span of labour, God has taken him by the hand and gathered him to himself).

The resemblance between the New Testament and the Talmudic versions of the parable is so striking that it can hardly be attributed to chance. It raises the question whether Jesus made use of a Jewish parable and recast it, or whether Rabbi Ze'era used a parable of Jesus, perhaps without being aware of its source. We can say with something approaching certainty that the priority belongs to Jesus, even apart from the fact Ze'era lived 300 years later. For the rabbinical version shows secondary traits (e.g. the owner of the vineyard has become a king), and has an artificial character (the king walks with the industrious labourer from eight a.m. till six p.m., that is for ten hours); but most significant is the feature that it is only with Jesus that the grumbling of the discontented labourers suits the situation in which the parable is told; it does not make sense at Rabbi Bun's funeral. The transformation that the parable has undergone in the mouth of the rabbinical scholar is all the more instructive. While in other respects the course of the story is substantially the same in both versions, they differ essentially on one point. In the rabbinical version the labourer who has worked only a short time has done more than all the rest; he has fully earned his wages, and the purpose of the parable is to extol his excellence. In Jesus' parable the labourers who were engaged last can show nothing to warrant a claim to a full day's wages, which they receive solely through the goodness of their employer. So there lies in this apparently trivial detail the difference between two worlds—the world of merit, and the world of grace; the law contrasted with the gospel.

The parable reflects the life of a period over which there brooded the spectre of unemployment.[1] As we have seen (see pp. 28f.), the parable, which was originally spoken to people who resembled the grumbling labourers, ended with the reproachful question (v. 15): 'Do you begrudge my generosity?' God acts like that householder who sympathized with the unemployed and their families. That is the way he acts now. He gives tax-collectors and sinners a share, all undeserved, in his salvation. So, too, he will deal with them on the last day. That, says Jesus, is what he is like; and because he is like that, so am I, as I am acting under his orders and in his stead. Are you going to grumble at God's goodness? That is the core of Jesus' vindication of the gospel: See what God is like—all goodness.

There still remains a number of parables devoted to this central thought, to which Jesus never wearied of returning. The *parable of the Pharisee and the Tax-collector* (Luke 18.9–14) is addressed, according to v. 9, 'to some who trusted in themselves [instead of in God] that they were righteous and despised others'—i.e. to the Pharisees. That the parable was addressed to them is confirmed by its content.

The language and content show that the parable belongs to an early Palestinian tradition. Verse 10: 'Two men': both live in Jerusalem (cf. v. 14, 'to his house'). 'Up into the temple': the temple is on high ground, with valleys to the south, east, and west. 'To pray': they go to the temple at the hour of prayer, i.e. at 3 p.m. (Acts 3.1). Verse 11: 'With himself' belongs to 'stood', as prayer was not usually silent, but was spoken under one's

[1] An example: Josephus tells of relief works in Jerusalem to give work to eighteen thousand unemployed after the building of the temple.

breath (like reading, see Acts 8.30). So the meaning is something like 'He took up a prominent position and said this prayer'. The prayer names in v. 11b the sins from which the Pharisee has refrained, and in v. 12 his good deeds. Although v. 12 has the form of an independent sentence, it depends logically on 'I thank thee'. He mentions two works that he is really in no way obliged to perform: (1) Whereas the law prescribes only one annual fast, namely the Day of Atonement, he fasts voluntarily twice a week, on Mondays and Thursdays, probably interceding for the people's sins. Anyone who is familiar with the East knows that, because of the heat, abstinence from drinking is the severest element in a fast. (2) He gives tithes of everything that he buys, so as to be sure of using nothing that has not been tithed, although corn, new wine, and oil should already have been tithed by the producer.[1] This was therefore a signal act of voluntary self-denial —he offered God not only his person but also his purse. Verse 13: The Greek word *telōnēs*, rendered 'tax-collector' by RSV and 'tax-gatherer' by NEB, rather designates a collector of customs. While the taxes, such as poll-tax and land-tax, were collected by state officials, the customs of a district were farmed out, probably to the highest bidder; so the collector of the customs saw himself as a businessman and tried to keep his profit as high as possible. Tariffs were, no doubt, fixed by the state, but the collectors did not lack devices for defrauding the public. In public opinion they were on a level with robbers; they possessed no civil rights and were shunned by all respectable people. 'Standing far off': in contrast to the Pharisee (v. 11) he remained standing at a distance. 'Would not' means 'did not venture to'. Beating the breast, or more accurately the heart (as the seat of sin), is an expression of the deepest contrition. Verse 14a: 'Justified' means here 'blessed with God's pleasure'. This passage is the only one in the Gospels where 'to justify' is used in a sense similar to that in which Paul generally uses it. But the construction is non-Pauline, so that Pauline influence is not to be assumed here; on the contrary, the passage shows that the Pauline doctrine of justification is rooted in the teaching of Jesus. The phrase 'rather than the other' is hardly intelligible; it is an

[1] Less probably (with the emphasis on 'all'): he went beyond what was prescribed, and tithed everything, even the garden-herbs such as mint, dill, cummin (Matt. 23.23), and rue (Luke 11.42). Or: he gives 10 per cent of his income for charitable purposes.

accurate translation of the Greek text, but the latter translates the original Aramaic too literally. If we proceed from the Aramaic, the meaning is: 'The latter went down to his house justified, but not the former.' In this way the passage is given its full severity. God was pleased with the tax-collector, but not with the Pharisee. Verse 14b contains a generalizing conclusion which affirms a favourite gospel theme, the eschatological reversal of existing conditions. It is in the form of an antithetic parallelism, describing God's dealings at the last judgment:[1] he will humble the proud, and exalt the humble.

To its first hearers the parable must have seemed shocking and incomprehensible. A prayer very similar to that of the Pharisee has come down to us from the first century AD in the Talmud: 'I thank thee, O Lord, my God, that thou hast given me my lot with those who sit in the house of learning, and not with those who sit at the street-corners; for I am early to work, and they are early to work, I am early to work on the words of the Torah, and they are early to work on things of no moment. I weary myself, and they weary themselves; I weary myself and profit thereby, and they weary themselves to no profit. I run, and they run; I run towards the life of the age to come, and they run towards the pit of destruction.'[2] We see from this that the Pharisee's prayer in Luke 18.11f. is taken from life; in fact, we have in this Jewish prayer an excellent commentary on the 'I thank thee' in Luke 18.11. The Pharisee does really give thanks for God's guidance. He is quite aware that he owes his other self—his better self—to 'his God', who has given him 'his lot' with those who take their religious duties seriously. He would not at any price change places with the other man, even though the latter is better off than he; for his way, wearisome as it is, holds the promise of 'the life of the age to come'. Has he not abundant cause for thanks-

[1] The passive 'will be humbled/will be exalted' is a circumlocution for the divine name, and the future is eschatological.
[2] Cf. also the Hymns Scroll from Qumran (1QH 7.34): 'I praise thee, O Lord, that thou has not allowed my lot to fall among the worthless community, nor assigned me a part in the circle of the secret ones.'

giving? We notice, too, that his prayer contains no petition, only thanks[1]—for 'the greatest blessing that man can desire, a foretaste of the world to come' (Jülicher). What fault can be found with his prayer? The tax-collector, too, must be viewed from the standpoint of his own time. He did not even venture, it is said, to lift up his eyes to heaven, to say nothing of his hands (so we must complete the description, for the uplifted hands were part of the usual gesture in prayer); but his head was bowed, and his hands were crossed on his breast. What follows is no part of the usual attitude in prayer; it is an outburst of despair. The man beats on his heart, wholly forgetting where he is, overwhelmed by the bitter sense of his distance from God. He and his family are in a hopeless position, since for him repentance involves not only the abandonment of his sinful way of life but also the restitution of his fraudulent gains plus an added fifth. How can he know everyone whom he has cheated? Not only his situation, but even his cry for mercy, is hopeless. And then comes the concluding sentence: 'I tell you, this man went down to his house justified, not the other' (v. 14a); God has forgiven him, and not forgiven the other! Such a conclusion must have come as a complete surprise to those who heard it; none of them had anticipated it. What fault had the Pharisee committed, and what had the tax-collector done by way of reparation? Leaving v. 14b out of account,[2] Jesus does not go into this question: he simply says: That is God's decision. He does, however, hint at the reason in God's apparent injustice. The tax-collector's urgent prayer is a quotation: he uses the opening words of Ps. 51, only adding (with an adversative sense) 'sinner'—'My God, have mercy on me, although I am so sinful' (v. 13). But we find in the same psalm: 'The sacrifice acceptable to God is a broken spirit; a broken and contrite heart, O God, thou wilt not despise' (v. 17). God's character, says Jesus, is such as is described in Ps. 51. He accepts the

---

[1] Verse 12 also belongs to the thanksgiving (see above).
[2] It cannot be decided with certainty whether v. 14b is original.

despairing, hopeless sinner, and rejects the self-righteous. He is the God of the despairing, and for the broken-hearted his mercy is boundless. That is what God is like, and that is how he is now acting through me as his representative.

Finally let us recall the *parable of the Two Debtors* (see pp. 98–100), one owing much and the other owing little, but both forgiven by their creditor (Luke 7.41–43). Surely a rare specimen among creditors! Where may such a one be found? Clearly Jesus was speaking of God, who is so inconceivably kind. Do you not understand, Simon? This woman's love, which you despise, is the expression of her boundless gratitude for God's inconceivable goodness. You wrong both her and me, and so you are missing God's best gift!

All the parables that deal with the gospel itself are a defence of the good news. The actual proclamation of the good news to sinners took a different form, in the offer of forgiveness, in Jesus' inviting the guilty to taste his hospitality, and in his calling them to follow him. It was not to sinners that he addressed the gospel parables, but to his critics, to those who rejected him because he gathered the despised around him. They were disappointed, because they were expecting a day of wrath; they closed their hearts to the good news, because in making up their minds to walk in God's way and to serve him with unfaltering piety, they had achieved too good an opinion of themselves. To these men the gospel was an offence, and it should be noticed that the offence was, all along, not that of the cross (I Cor. 1.23), but of something that preceded the cross, namely the humble appearance of the messianic community—a point of some importance in relation to authenticity. Again and again they ask: Why do you associate with this riff-raff that is shunned by all respectable people? And he replies: Because they are sick, and need me, because they are truly repentant, and because they feel the gratitude of children forgiven by God; and because you, with your loveless, self-righteous, disobedient hearts, reject the gospel. But above all, because God is like that, so kind to the poor, so glad when the lost are found, so full of a father's love for the child who has gone wrong, so merciful to the despairing, the helpless, and the needy. That is why!

## 3 The Great Assurance

This group of parables, to which there belong on the one hand the four contrasting parables (the Mustard-seed, the Leaven, the Sower, and the Patient Husbandman), and on the other hand those of the Unjust Judge and the Man asking for Help by Night, contains one of the central elements of Jesus' preaching.

The *parables of the Mustard-seed* (Mark 4.30–32; Matt. 13.31f.; Luke 13.18f.; Gospel of Thomas 20) and *the Leaven* (Matt. 13.33; Luke 13.20f.; Gospel of Thomas 96) are so closely related in content that they can well be discussed together, although they may have been spoken on separate occasions (see p. 72 above).

In the Gospel of Thomas the two parables appear as follows: 'The disciples said to Jesus, "Tell us what the Kingdom of Heaven is like". He said to them, "It is like a mustard-seed, smaller than all seeds. But when it falls on the tilled earth, it puts forth a great branch and becomes a shelter for the birds of heaven" ' (Gospel of Thomas 20). 'Jesus said, "The Kingdom of Heaven is like a woman. She took a little leaven, hid it in dough, and made large loaves of it. He that has ears, let him hear" ' (Gospel of Thomas 96).

Both parables show a strongly marked Palestinian colouring. To understand them, we have to recognize that the translation 'The Kingdom of Heaven is like a grain of mustard-seed' or 'like a little leaven' is misleading; we have, in fact, two parables here with a datival introduction (see pp. 79f.), which should be rendered, 'It is the case with

the Kingdom of God as with a grain of mustard-seed', or
'as with a little leaven'. The purpose of the parables is to
compare the Kingdom of God with the final stage of the
process there described—with the tall shrub giving shelter
to the birds, and with the mass of dough wholly permeated
by the leaven; the tree that shelters the birds is a common
metaphor for a mighty kingdom that protects its vassals,
and the dough in Rom. 11.16 is a metaphor for God's people.

Both parables depict a sharp contrast. This agreement in
pattern was the reason why both Matthew (13.31–33) and
Luke (13.18–21) kept them as a double parable. Thus we are
shown the mustard-seed, as big as a pin's head, about
the smallest thing one can see, 'the smallest of all the seeds
on earth' (Mark 4.31)—every word emphasizes its smallness
—and when it has grown, it is 'the greatest of all shrubs,
and puts forth large branches, so that the birds of the air
can make nests in its shade' (v. 32)—every word brings out
the size of the shrub, which, by the Lake of Gennesaret,
reaches a height of about eight to ten feet. Again we are
shown a scrap of leaven (I Cor. 5.6; Gal. 5.9), absurdly
small in comparison with the great mass of more than a
bushel of meal. In the evening, the housewife kneads it
into the dough, covers it with a cloth, leaves the mass to
stand overnight; and when she comes back to it in the
morning the whole mass of dough is leavened. It is not
the purpose of either parable merely to describe a process;
that would be the way of the western mind. The Oriental
thinks in a different way; he looks at the first stage and the
last, seizing the paradoxical element in both cases, the two
successive, yet fundamentally different, situations. It is no
mere coincidence that in the Talmud (b. Sanh. 90b), in Paul
(I Cor. 15.35–38), in John (12.24), and in I Clement (24.4–5),
the seed is the image of resurrection, the symbol of the
mystery of life out of death. The oriental mind sees two
wholly different situations: on the one hand the dead seed,
on the other the waving cornfield; here death, there, through
the divine creative power, life. 'Let us take the crops: how

and in what way does the sowing take place? The sower
went out and cast each of the seeds on to the ground. They
fall on the field, parched and bare, and suffer decay; then
from their decay the greatness of the Master's providence
raises them up; one grain becomes many, and they bring
forth fruit' (I Clem. 24.4–5). The modern man, passing
through the ploughed field, thinks of what is going on
beneath the soil, and sees a biological development. The
people of the Bible, passing through the same ploughed
field, look up and see one of God's miracles after another,
nothing less than resurrection from the dead. That is how
Jesus' audience understood the parables of the Mustard-
seed and the Leaven, as parables of contrast. Their meaning
is that out of the most insignificant beginnings, which are
a mere nothing to the human eye, God creates his mighty
Kingdom, which will embrace all the peoples of the
world.

If that is right, the occasion of the utterance of the two
parables may be taken as an expression of doubt concerning Jesus' mission. How different were the beginnings of
the messianic age, announced by Jesus, from what was
commonly expected! Could this wretched band, comprising
so many ill-reputed characters, be the wedding-guests of
God's redeemed community? Yes, says Jesus, it is. With
the same compelling certainty with which a tall shrub
grows out of a tiny mustard-seed, or a little leaven produces
a fermenting mass of dough, God's miraculous power will
turn my small band into the mighty host of God's people in
the messianic age, embracing the Gentiles. 'Is not this why
you are wrong, that you know neither the scriptures nor
the power of God?' (Mark 12.24).

If we are to grasp fully the impact of this statement of
Jesus, we must add one final point. His hearers were familiar
with the simile of the high tree, taken from the Scripture
(Ezek. 31; Dan. 4) where it symbolizes world-power, and
with that of the tiny quantity of leaven which leavens a
mass of dough, taken from the interpretation of the Pass-

over, as a symbol of malice and wickedness.[1] Jesus was bold enough to use both similes in the opposite sense, and apply them, not to the powers of Satan, but to the royal majesty of God.

To understand the *parable of the Sower* (Mark 4.3–8; Matt. 13.3–8; Luke 8.5–8; Gospel of Thomas 9; see p. 20 above) in what was probably its original meaning, we must reject the interpretation that misses its eschatological point, shifts its emphasis from the eschatological to the psychological and hortatory aspect, and turns it into a warning to the converted against a failure to stand fast in time of persecution, and against worldliness (see p. 64).[2] The understanding of the parable depends on the recognition of the fact that its beginning describes a different point of time from its end. First we have a general description of the sowing, but in the last verse it is already harvest-time. Again we have a contrast-parable; on the one hand there is a description of the many frustrations to which the sower's labour is exposed; that is the only reason why the as yet unploughed fallow land (see p. 9) is described; Jesus could have gone on to mention the scorching wind (sirocco), locusts, and other enemies of the seed; the Gospel of Thomas (9) does, in fact, mention the worm.[3] In contrast to this, the parable shows us the ripening field with its rich harvest—for we must not consider v. 8 as a description of a specially fruitful part of the field (as in the interpretation, vv. 14–20), but of the whole field at the moment of harvest. The coming of God's Kingdom is compared, as so often, to the harvest (see pp. 92f.). The abnormal tripling, after the oriental fashion, of the harvest's yield (thirty-, sixty-, a hundredfold) signifies the eschatological abundance of God, surpassing all human measure (v. 8). To human eyes much of the labour may seem futile and fruitless, resulting

[1] I Cor. 5.6–8.
[2] The parable's title 'The Fourfold Field' (arising from its interpretation) is misleading; cf. p. 101 n. 1.
[3] 'And other seeds fell on the thorns; they choked the seeds, and the worm ate them' (see p. 20 above).

apparently in frequent failure; but Jesus is full of joyful confidence: God's hour is coming, and will bring with it a harvest of reward beyond all asking and understanding. In spite of every failure and opposition, God brings from hopeless beginnings the glorious end that he has promised. Once again it is not difficult to visualize the situation that caused Jesus to speak the parable: it is no doubt closely related to that which called forth the parables of the Mustard-seed and the Leaven—doubts about the success of the gospel message. Here, however, they were not occasioned, as they were there, by the meagreness of Jesus' following, but by the apparently ineffective preaching (Mark 6.5f.), the bitter hostility (Mark 3.6), and the increasing number of desertions (John 6.60). Did not all this contradict the claims of his mission? Consider the husbandman, says Jesus; he might well despair in view of the many adverse factors that destroy and threaten his seed. 'O men of little faith' (Matt. 6.30); 'Have you no faith?' (Mark 4.40).

Finally, to the parables of contrast there belongs the *parable of the Seed growing secretly*, which might more accurately be called the *parable of the Patient Husbandman* (Mark 4.26–29). Once more the coming of God's Kingdom is compared to the harvest.[1] Again we are confronted with a sharp contrast; the inactivity of the farmer after sowing is graphically described: his life follows its ordered round of sleeping and waking, night and day; without his being able to explain it or do anything about it, the seed grows from stalk to ear, and from ear to ripened corn. Then, suddenly, the moment arrives which rewards the patient waiting. The corn is ripe, the sickle is thrust in, the joyful cry rings out, 'The harvest has come'. So it is with the Kingdom of God: with the same certainty as the harvest that comes for the husbandman after his long waiting, God, when his hour has come, when the eschatological term (v. 29; cf. Joel 3.13) is complete, brings in the last judgment and the Kingdom. Man can do nothing about it except wait patiently, as the

[1] Not to the seed. Cf. the reference in Mark 4.29b, c to Joel 3.13.

farmer does (James 5.7). It has often been supposed that this parable was intended as a contrast to the efforts of the Zealots to bring in the messianic deliverance by forcibly throwing off the Roman yoke, and here it must be remembered that the circle of the disciples included ex-Zealots.[1] Why did Jesus not act when action was what the hour demanded? Why did he not take vigorous steps to purge out the sinners and establish the purified community (Matt. 13.24–30; see pp. 177f.)? Why did he not give the signal to free Israel from the Gentile yoke (Mark 12.14 par.; [John] 8.5f.)? Did not this refusal of Jesus deny the claim of his mission? Once again it is a contrast-parable by which Jesus replied to the doubts about his mission, and to disappointed hopes. Think of the farmer, he says, who patiently awaits the time of the harvest. So, too, God's hour comes irresistibly. He made the decisive beginning, the seed has been sown. He leaves nothing undone (cf. Phil. 1.6). His beginning guarantees the end. Till then, we must wait in patience and not try to anticipate God, but in full confidence leave everything to him.

The feature common to all four parables is that they contrast the beginning with the end, and what a contrast! The insignificance of the beginning, and the triumph of the end! But the contrast is not the whole truth. The fruit is the result of the seed, and the end is implicit in the beginning. The infinitely great is already active in the infinitely small. In the present, and indeed in secret, the event is already in motion. The undisclosed nature of God's Kingdom is a matter of faith in a world which as yet knows nothing of it. Those to whom it has been given to understand the mystery of the Kingdom (Mark 4.11) can already see in its hidden and insignificant beginnings the coming glory of God.

This unwavering assurance is an essential element in Jesus' preaching: God's hour is coming; indeed, it has

---

[1] It may not be accidental that in Mark 3.18f. par. Matt. 10.4 Simon the Zealot and (probably) Judas Iscariot are named together as a couple cf. Mark 6.7).

already begun. In his beginning the end is already implicit. No doubts with regard to his mission, no scorn, no lack of faith, no impatience, can make Jesus waver in his certainty that out of a mere nothing, despite all failure, God is carrying his beginnings on to completion. All that is necessary is to take God seriously, to take him into account in spite of all outward appearance.

On what grounds does this confidence rest? The answer to this question is to be found in two closely related parables. First, the *parable of the Unjust Judge* (Luke 18.2–8).

On v. 1 see p. 123. Verse 2: The description 'the unrighteous judge' (v. 6) seems intended to characterize the judge as corrupt, and v. 2 is to be understood similarly. '. . . nor regarded man': he does not care in the least what people say about him. Verse 3: The widow need not be regarded as an old woman; the early marriageable age (between 13 and 14 for girls) meant that widows might be quite young. Since she brings her case to a single judge, and not to a tribunal, it seems to be a money matter—a debt, a pledge, or part of an inheritance, is being withheld from her. She is too poor to bribe the judge (in the Old Testament widows and orphans are already standing types of the helpless and defenceless); her opponent in this case is to be thought of as a rich and influential man; hence persistence is her only weapon. Verse 4: 'He refused': this has the same meaning as in Mark 6.26 and Luke 18.13, 'he would not venture' (*sc.* because of her opponent's influential position). Verse 5: Finally he yields 'because this widow bothers me' (gets on my nerves; 'this' is depreciatory, as in 15.30). 'Or she will wear me out by her continual coming': it is not the fear of an outburst of rage on the woman's part that makes him give way, but her persistence; he is tired of her perpetual nagging, and wants to be left in peace.[1] This, as we shall see, is the only rendering that

---

[1] H. B. Tristram, *Eastern Customs in Bible Lands*, London, 1894, p. 228, gives a very vivid description of the judicial court at Nisibis (Mesopotamia). Opposite the entrance sat the Cadi, half buried in cushions, and surrounded by secretaries. The front of the hall was crowded with people, each demanding that his case should be heard first. The wiser ones whispered to the secretaries and slipped bribes across to them, and had their business despatched quickly. In the

makes the application in vv. 7–8a intelligible. Verse 7 is rather difficult in its construction; according to the sense it may be translated somewhat as follows: 'Will not God hasten to rescue his elect who cry to him day and night, even if he puts their patience to the test?' Verse 8a: 'Speedily' means here that he will help them 'suddenly', 'unexpectedly'. Verse 8b: The parable ends on an unexpected note of profound gravity: 'Nevertheless, when the Son of man comes, will he find faith on earth?'

Luke clearly links this parable with that of the Pharisee and the Tax-collector as intended to give guidance about the right way to pray (cf. 18.1): prayer should be persistent and humble. But the parable of the Pharisee and the Tax-collector is far from being a lesson on how to pray; and the same may be said about the parable under discussion, in spite of its introductory verse (18.1), which has Lukan peculiarities. On this interpretation the widow is the central figure, whereas Jesus' interpretation (vv. 6–8a) shows that he intended to direct attention to the figure of the judge.[1] Why did Jesus tell the story? He gives the answer himself in vv. 7–8a: he expected his hearers to apply to God the conclusion about the judge. If this inconsiderate man, who has been refusing to hear the widow's case, finally gives heed to her distress, even after long delay, merely to rid himself of her incessant pestering, how much more will God! God listens to the cry of the poor with unwearied patience; they are his elect, he is moved with compassion for their need, and suddenly he intervenes for their deliverance. If the parable, as we may

---

meantime a poor woman broke through the orderly proceedings with loud cries for justice. She was sternly bidden to be quiet, and reproachfully told that she came every day. 'And so I will do,' she loudly exclaimed, 'until the Cadi hears my case.' At length, at the end of the session, the Cadi impatiently asked, 'What does the woman want?' Her story was soon told. The tax-collector was demanding payment from her, although her only son was on military service. The case was quickly decided, and her patience was rewarded. If she had had money to pay a clerk, she would have obtained justice much sooner. It is an exact modern analogy to Luke 18.2ff.

[1] Hence the usual designation of the parable as the parable of the Importunate Widow is unsuitable (cf. p. 101 n. 1).

assume from v. 8b, is addressed to the disciples, it was clearly
called forth by their grief and anxiety in the time of tribulation that Jesus had depicted for them with absolute
clarity—persecutions, injuries, denunciations, trials, martyrdom, and final temptations to lose their faith when Satan
is manifested. This has already begun. Who can endure to
the end? Have no anxiety in the face of persecution, says
Jesus; you are God's elect, and he will hear your cry. By the
intervention of his holy will he will even shorten the time of
tribulation (Mark 13.20). There is no doubting his power,
goodness, and help. That is the final certainty. Your concern
should be with a different matter: when the Son of man
comes, will he find faith on the earth?

Almost a doublet of the parable of the Unjust Judge is
that of *the Friend who was asked for Help at Night* (Luke
11.5–8).[1]

The parable gives a vivid description of conditions in a
Palestinian village. Verse 5: There are no shops, and before sunrise the housewife bakes the day's supply of bread for the family;
but it is generally known in the village who has still some bread
left in the evening. Even today three loaves are regarded as a
meal for one person. He only intends to borrow them and soon
replace them. Verse 6: It is an imperative duty in the East to
entertain a guest. Verse 7: The neighbour's annoyance at being
disturbed is expressed at once in his omission of the address
(otherwise in v. 5). 'Now' = 'long ago' (as, e.g., in John 19.28);
the Oriental goes to bed early. In the evening the house is dark;
the little oil lamp that burns through the night gives only a
glimmer. 'The door was shut long ago'—that means locked and
bolted. The bolt is a wooden or iron bar pushed through rings in
the door-panels; drawing the bolt is a tiresome and very noisy
business. 'And my children are with me in bed': we have to
think of a peasant's house consisting of only one room,[2] in the
raised part of which the whole family slept on a mat; they would
therefore all be disturbed if the father had to get up and unbolt

---

[1] The usual designation of the parable as the parable of the Importunate Friend is misleading; see p. 101 n. 1.
[2] Thus, too, in Matt. 5.15.

the door. 'I cannot get up': 'I can't' means, as it so often does, 'I won't'. Verse 8: 'Surely, even if he will not get up and give him what he asks for friendship's sake, yet he will get up and give him, because of his importunity [an alternative translation, based on the supposed original Aramaic text, is: for the sake of his (own) shamelessness, i.e. so as not to lose face in the matter], as much as he needs.'

Luke has transmitted the parable in the context of the instruction about prayer in 11.1–13, and therefore understood it to be an exhortation to unwearied prayer, as 11.9–13 plainly shows; but this context is, as in other cases, secondary, and should therefore not be taken as a starting-point for an attempt to set out the parable's original meaning. That meaning should rather be sought in the recognition that 'Which of you?' (11.5) in the New Testament regularly introduces questions that expect the emphatic answer 'No one. Impossible.' or 'Everyone, of course.' This 'Which of you?' would best be rendered by 'Can you imagine that any of you would?' (Matt. 6.27 par. Luke 12.25; Matt. 7.9 par. Luke 11.11; Matt. 12.11 par. Luke 14.5; Luke 14.28; 15.4; 17.7). But in that case, the question cannot possibly end with v. 6, because v. 6 only describes the situation, and does not insistently demand a reply. Verses 5–7 should therefore be regarded as one continuous rhetorical question: 'Can you imagine that, if one of you had a friend who came to you at midnight and said to you, "My friend, lend me three loaves, because a friend of mine has come to me on a journey, and I have nothing to set before him", you would call out, "Don't disturb me . . ."? Can you imagine such a thing?' The answer would be: 'Unthinkable! In no circumstances would he leave his friend's request unanswered.' So it is only if we understand v. 7 as describing, not the refusal of a request, but the utter impossibility of such a refusal, that the parable is in accordance with the common rules of oriental hospitality, and its real point becomes clear. For the result of taking vv. 5–7 as a single connected question is that v. 8 is seen to be no longer concerned with the neighbour's reiterated request, but solely with the motive that actuates the friend to whom he is applying for help: if he will not grant the request for friendship's sake, he will at least do it to rid himself of the importunity (or: so as not to appear disobliging). Thus v. 8 simply re-emphasizes the unthinkable nature of the suggestion, so that the central figure is not the petitioner (as in the Lukan context), but the friend who is roused from sleep. The parable is concerned, not with the petitioner's importunity, but with the certainty that the petition will be granted. It is clear, then, that the parable, like that of the Unjust Judge, expects the hearers to draw a conclusion from the lesser to the greater. If the friend, roused from sleep at night, hastens without a moment's delay to fulfil the request of a neighbour in difficulty, even though the whole family must be disturbed by the drawing of the bolt, how much more will God be willing to act! He hears the cry of the needy, and comes to their help. He does more than they ask. On that you may rely in all confidence.

With these two parables of the Judge, and the Friend asked for Help at Night, both of which express confidence that God will hear the appeal of his own when they cry to him in their need, we should connect the short saying: 'For every one who asks receives' (Matt. 7.8 = Luke 11.10). This aphorism evidently springs from the experience of the beggar: he has only to persist, to take no refusal, to be undeterred by abuse, and he will receive a gift. Every visitor to the East can tell stories of the persistence of oriental beggars.[1] Jesus applies the beggar's wisdom to the disciples. If the beggar, although harshly repulsed at first, knows that persistent appeals will open the hands of his hard-hearted fellow-men, how much more certain should you be that your

[1] Incidentally, this pertinacity is not mere greed, but has deeper reasons: on the one hand, the poor are specially protected by divine law, and have therefore a divinely guaranteed right to the gift; so the beggar's 'calling' is by no means to be despised; on the other hand, the beggar is so pertinacious because he needs the gift in order that he himself also may have the power to do good; we read in the Talmud: 'Even a poor man who lives by alms may be charitable.'

persistence in prayer will open the hands of your heavenly Father.

The four contrast-parables and the two with which we have just been occupied were, if our interpretation is right, called forth by different occasions. Whereas the contrast-parables express Jesus' confidence in the face of doubt concerning his mission, the parables of the Judge and the Friend are intended to make the disciples certain that God will deliver them from the coming tribulation. Nonetheless, the two groups of parables are very closely related. In both there is the same unwavering trust; in both Jesus says: Take God seriously; he works wonders, and his mercy for his own is the most certain thing of all.

## 4 In Sight of Disaster

Jesus' message not only proclaims salvation, but also announces judgment; it is a warning and a call to repentance in view of the terrible urgency of the crisis. The number of parables in this category is, indeed, alarming. Over and over again Jesus raised his voice in warning, striving to open the eyes of a blinded people.

That the little *parable of the Children in the Market-place* (Matt. 11.16f. par. Luke 7.31f.) belongs to the early stage of the tradition is shown already by the excessively hostile estimate of Jesus which is contained in v. 19a. The denigration of him as 'a glutton and a drunkard' comes from Deut. 21.20, and stigmatizes him on the strength of this connection as a 'stubborn and rebellious' son who deserved to be stoned. In reply Jesus says: You are like the children in the streets, shouting at their companions, 'Spoilsports! Spoilsports! We played the flute, but you would not dance. We sang the funeral dirge, but you would not beat your breasts.' (Matt. 11.17; Luke 7.32). 'We wanted to play at

weddings', shout the boys to their playmates (the round dance
at a wedding is the men's dance), 'but you wouldn't.' 'We
wanted to play at funerals, but you wouldn't play', cry the
girls to their playfellows (the mourning dirge is for the
women).

And you, says Jesus, are just like those domineering and
disagreeable children, who blame their companions for
being spoilsports because they will not dance to their piping.
God sends his messengers, the last messengers, to the last
generation before the catastrophe. But all you do is to give
orders and criticize. You say that the Baptist is mad
because he fasts while you want to make merry; and you
scold me because I eat with tax-collectors while you insist
on strict separation from sinners. Neither the preaching
of repentance nor the proclamation of the gospel suits you.
So you cavil at God's messengers, 'while Rome is burning'
(C. H. Dodd). Can you not see that wisdom is justified by
her deeds (Matt. 11.19)—that the deeds, the signs that the
decisive moment has arrived, are God's vindication? That
the call to repentance and the preaching of the good news
are God's very last and final warnings?

How blind you are! You can read the signs of the weather,
but you cannot recognize the signs of the time (Luke
12.54–56). 'Wherever the body is, there the eagles will be
gathered together' (Matt. 24.28 par. Luke 17.37). They do
not circle 'over empty space' (Bishop Lilje); they scent the
prey. Do you not see that there is something in the air? No,
you are like a house whose rooms are dark because their
source of light has failed. You are blind; you are hardened
(Matt. 6.22f.; Luke 11.34–36). You feast and dance—and
the volcano may erupt at any moment. The horrible fate
of Sodom and Gomorrha will be repeated (Luke 17.28f.).
The deluge is at hand (Matt. 24.37–39; Luke 17.26f.).[1]

The coupling of the deluge of fire with that of water also lies
behind the double metaphor in Luke 12.49f.: 'I came to cast fire

[1] Cf. also Matt. 7.24–27 par. Luke 6.47–49.

upon the earth; and would that it were already kindled! I have a baptism to be baptized with; and how I am constrained until it is accomplished!' In this double metaphor we have an echo of that tragic conflict whose intensity has no parallel in the Bible except in the self-revelations of the prophet Jeremiah, the conflict of the imperative call of his mission and the reluctance of natural affections. Jesus is the bringer-in of the new age; but the way to new creation lies through disaster and destruction, through the deluge of fire and water. 'He who is near me is near the fire; he who is far from me is far from the Kingdom.'[1]

God's curse lies on the barren fig-tree (Luke 13.7); it is cut down and thrown into the fire (Matt. 7.19). The fate of the dry tree will be more terrible than that of the green tree (Luke 23.31). Calamity will overtake you as un-expectedly as the snare catches the unwary bird (Luke 21.34f.). The simile of the traveller gives warning that there are only twelve hours in the day. There is only a little day-light left before night comes, when the traveller stumbles on the stony paths and loses his way in the dark (John 12.35; cf. 11.9f.). Take warning from the householder who lay sound asleep while his house was burgled (Matt. 24.43f.; Luke 12.39f.; Gospel of Thomas 21b).[2] Listen to the *story of the Rich Fool* (Luke 12.16–20; Gospel of Thomas 63[3]) who, after a rich harvest, prepared for a richer one, and whose security God shattered in a night.

In Luke an introductory dialogue (vv. 13–15) provides the occasion for the parable. The younger of two brothers complains that the elder refuses to give him his share of the inheritance.[4] The

---

[1] A saying of Jesus that is not in the New Testament, but is in the Gospel of Thomas (saying 82). Cf. J. Jeremias, *Unknown Sayings of Jesus*, second English edition, London, 1964, pp. 66–73.

[2] See pp. 37f.

[3] Jesus said, "There was a rich man, who had great possessions. He said: 'I will use my possessions to sow, to reap, to plant, and to fill my barns with the produce, so that I shall lack nothing.' That is what he thought in his heart. And in that night he died. He who has ears, let him hear!' '

[4] The elder brother would rather leave the inheritance undivided.

fact that he appealed to Jesus, although the latter was a layman, shows what prestige Jesus enjoyed among the people (v. 13). Jesus refuses to give a decision, not merely because he disclaims any authority to do so (v. 14), but primarily because the possession of property is irrelevant to the life of the age to come (v. 15). The parable explains why he regards earthly wealth as wholly negligible. This dialogue (vv. 13f., but without the saying in v. 15) is preserved in the Gospel of Thomas 72 as an independent fragment, so it will not originally have belonged to the parable. Verse 18: Here 'barns' 'does not mean barns where corn can be kept till it is threshed, but warehouses or stores in which later on the grain can be laid up' (W. Michaelis). Verse 20: 'But God said to him': God sent him a message (perhaps in a dream through the angel of death). 'Your soul is required of you' = 'God will require your soul': life is a loan from God, who declares that its return is to be demanded that very night.

This rich farmer, who thinks that he need not fear bad harvests for many a year (v. 19), is a fool (v. 20)—that is, according to the biblical meaning of the word, a man who in practice denies God's existence (Ps. 14.1). He does not take God into account, and fails to see the sword of Damocles, the threat of death, hanging over his head. Here we have to avoid a too obvious conclusion. We are not to think that Jesus intended to impress on his audience the old truth that death strikes unexpectedly. Rather do the appeals and warning parables, taken together, show that he regarded as the impending danger, not the inevitable death of the individual, but the approaching eschatological catastrophe and judgment. That is the case here; Luke 12.16–20 is an eschatological parable, whose conclusion Jesus expected his hearers to apply to their own situation: we are just as foolish as the rich fool under the threat of death, if we heap up possessions when the deluge is threatening.

---

Such a jointly held inheritance is praised by the Psalmist (Ps. 133.1: 'Behold, how good and pleasant it is when brothers dwell in unity'), and is presupposed, e.g., in Matt. 6.24 (see p. 152 n. 3).

What will happen? First comes the preliminary attack, when the jackal who feeds on corpses, seeks, after devouring the Baptist, to attack the Son of man (Luke 13.32). Then comes the great hour of temptation, the final assault of the evil one, destruction of the temple, and unspeakable calamity (Luke 23.29), and after that, God's judgment. The hour of separation comes. The distinction between wise and foolish maidens, between faithful and unfaithful stewards, will become apparent; the hearers of the word will be separated from the doers, and the sheep from the goats; there will be two in the field, two at the mill, men there, women here, outwardly alike, to human eyes indistinguishable; but the moment of separation will reveal the terrible contrast—one a child of God, the other a child of destruction (Matt. 24.40f.).

It is a characteristic of the numerous parables concerned with the coming judgment, that many of them address a warning to quite definite groups of people. Against Jesus' opponents there is the parable of the claimant to the throne,[1] as may be inferred from Luke 19.12, 14f., 17, 19, 27. The parables of the Servant entrusted with Supervision (Matt. 24.45–51a; Luke 12.42–46),[2] of the Pounds or the Talents (Matt. 25.14–30; Luke 19.12–27),[3] and of the Doorkeeper (Mark 13.33–37; Luke 12.35–38),[4] are addressed, as we have seen, apparently to the leaders of the people, especially to the scribes. God has entrusted them with much—the spiritual leadership of the nation, the knowledge of his will, the key to the Kingdom of God. Now God's judgment is at hand; now it will be decided whether the theologians have justified or abused his great trust, whether they have made good use of his gift or turned it to their own advantage and to the imposition of burdens on their fellow-men, whether they have opened the door of the Kingdom of God, or shut it. Their judgment will be specially severe. In the simile of the two servants (Luke 12.47–48a) Jesus tells them that he who knows the will of

[1] Pp. 46f.    [2] Pp. 44f.    [3] Pp. 45ff.    [4] Pp. 41ff.

God will be more severely punished than the common
people who do not know the law. The evangelists tell us
that the parable of the Wicked Husbandmen (Mark 12.1ff.
par.)[1] was addressed to the members of the Sanhedrin
(11.27 par.). This may well be correct. In the Song of the
Vineyard (Isa. 5.1ff.) to which Jesus refers, God's people are
compared to the vineyard, since the vineyard had been
the usual symbol of Israel;[2] and it may be assumed that,
as Jesus is not speaking about the vineyard, but about its
tenants, he is not referring to the people as a whole, but to
its leaders. Moreover, it is very possible that the parable
was spoken in connection with the cleansing of the temple,
as the present context says. In that case it would be the
temple authorities, especially the priestly members of the
Sanhedrin, to whom the parable's terrible threat refers. The
house of God has become a den of thieves. God, who has
waited with such immense patience, is now about to demand
his dues, and the last generation must expiate the accumula-
ted guilt.

According to Matt. 15.12, the saying about the blind
leaders of the blind, the leaders and the led who all fall into
the ditch together, applies to the Pharisees (Matt. 15.14;
Luke 6.39; Gospel of Thomas 34). Moreover, the related
metaphor of the mote and the beam (Matt. 7.3–5; Luke
6.41f.; Gospel of Thomas 26) was originally addressed to
them, and according to Matt. 12.33 the saying about the
good and evil trees (par. Matt. 7.16–20; Luke 6.43f.), to
which the metaphor of the good and evil treasure (Matt.
12.35; Luke 6.45; Gospel of Thomas 45b) provides a
counterpart, was also directed at them: Your acts and words
show that you are essentially evil, and lie under God's
judgment. Similarly, according to John 9.40 (cf. 10.6,
19–21), the parable of the Shepherd was addressed to the
Pharisees. It charges the leaders of the people with destroy-
ing God's flock like thieves and robbers; the coming of the
Good Shepherd has exposed their destructive activities.

[1] Pp. 57ff.      [2] Isa. 27.2–6; Jer. 12.10; Ps. 80.8–17.

It is over the capital that the lament in Matt. 23.37 par. Luke 13.34, the saying about the hen and her chickens, is uttered. The reference is to Isa. 31.5: 'Like birds hovering, so the Lord of hosts will protect Jerusalem; he will protect and deliver it, he will spare and rescue it.' In a bold metaphor, God is here compared to fluttering birds protecting their young. Jesus transfers the simile to himself, as God's appointed representative. Before the oncoming destruction that threatened Jerusalem like the swoop of an attacking bird of prey on a clutch of chickens, Jesus has watched, longing to overshadow, deliver, spare, and protect. 'And you would not.' Now God has forsaken the temple that you have desecrated, and has abandoned it and you to judgment (Matt. 23.38; Luke 13.35).

Finally, the parable of the Fig-tree (Luke 13.6–9) and the threat implied in *the saying about the salt that has become useless* and is cast into the street and trodden under foot (Matt. 5.13; Luke 14.34f.; cf. Mark 9.50a) are directed against Israel as a whole. To belong to God's people will not serve as a protection against God's judgment.

The strange expression 'If the salt becomes foolish' (Matt. 5.13; Luke 14.34)[1] rests on a mistranslation. In Mark it is translated correctly 'If salt becomes saltless' (9.50); the tradition on which Matthew and Luke depend, translating 'If the salt becomes foolish', clearly thought of the saying as referring to the foolish disciples, or to foolish Israel. It is to be assumed that Jesus, in using the expression 'salt that has become saltless' made use of a popular saying, indicating something useless or meaningless. 'Wherewith shall it be salted?' (Matt. 5.13, AV) probably does not mean 'Through what shall it [the salt] regain its saltness?' (see Mark 9.50), but 'With what are [the foods] to be salted?' (Luke 14.34 according to the Greek text). 'Except' (Matt. 5.13) does not express an exception, but is rather used adversatively ('but'; cf. Luke 4.26, 27; Matt. 12.4; Gal. 1.19): salt that has become saltless is of no further use, but will be cast out into the

---

[1] This is the literal rendering of the Greek which in RSV appears as 'if the salt has lost its taste'.

street. To the question in what circumstances in the daily life of Jesus' audience might salt become saltless and be cast out into the street, the usual answer is that Arab bakers sometimes cover the floor of their ovens with slabs of salt whose catalytic effect on the poorly burning fuel (e.g. dried camel-dung) might promote combustion; after about fifteen years this catalytic effect wears out, and the salt is thrown into the street. But this explanation overlooks the fact that the saying is clearly concerned with salt used as food (see above). So we must keep to the simpler explanation, based on everyday experience and reminding us that salt was obtained, not by any industrial process, but from evaporated pools by the shore of the Dead Sea, or from the small lakes on the edge of the Syrian desert, which dry up in summer. This salt crust, dug up from the surface of the soil, is never pure, but contains other things (magnesia, lime, vegetable remains) which, when the salt is dissolved by moisture, remain as useless refuse. Whereas Matthew and Mark take the saying about salt as addressed to the disciples, Luke regards it as a warning addressed to the crowd (14.25). This view may well be nearer the mark, for in the Talmud the saying about salt is taken as a threat spoken against Israel. Jesus is warning them that their being God's people is no ground for false confidence.

The last generation of the chosen people, the Messiah's generation, is the one on which the fateful decision will fall; it will either bear the burden of the common guilt (Matt. 23.35; Luke 11.50; cf. Mark 12.9) or become the recipient of complete forgiveness (Luke 19.42). But Jesus' most urgent warning of disaster was addressed to the messianic community, among whom, too, the final separation was to be effected. Two of his followers build themselves a house; no outward difference is apparent. But the flood of the final tribulation reveals that one had built his house on the rock, and the other on the sand (Matt. 7.24–27; Luke 6.47–49).

To understand the parables, it is necessary to realize that each was spoken in a particular concrete situation. It was not their purpose to propound moral precepts, but to shock into a realization of its danger a nation rushing into its own destruction—and especially its leaders, the theologians and priests. But above all, they were a call to repentance.


## 5 *It May Be Too Late*

It is the last hour. God's gracious rule has come. But the deluge is still at the door (Matt. 24.37–39; cf. 7.24–27); the axe lies at the root of the barren fig-tree. But God, marvellously suspending the fulfilment of his holy will, has allowed yet one more respite for repentance (*parable of the Fig-tree*, Luke 13.6–9), even as he can again, in the last extremity, suspend the fulfilment of his holy will and shorten, for the elects' sake, the time of the Antichrist's power (Mark 13.20).

Luke 13.6: 'In this vineyard': in Palestine, vineyards are generally planted with fruit-trees too, and are therefore orchards. Verse 7: The first three years of a fig-tree's growth were allowed to elapse before its fruit became clean (Lev. 19.23), and so six years had already passed since it was planted; thus it was hopelessly barren. 'Why should it use up the ground?': a fig-tree absorbs a specially large amount of nourishment, and so takes away sustenance needed by surrounding vines. Verse 8: 'And put on manure': manuring a vineyard is not mentioned in any passage of the Old Testament; moreover, the ordinary fig-tree needs no such care as a matter of duty. The gardener is therefore proposing to do something unusual, to take the last possible measures. In the story of Achiqar (before the fifth century BC) the words occur: 'My son, you are like a tree that yielded no fruit, although it stood by the water; and its owner was obliged to cut it down. And it said to him, "Transplant me, and if even then I bear no fruit, cut me down." But its owner said to it, "When you stood by the water you bore no fruit; how then will you bear fruit if you stand in another place?"' Jesus uses this folk-tale, which was probably current in various versions, but he gives it another ending: the request is not refused, but granted;

an announcement of judgment becomes a call to repentance. God's mercy goes so far as to grant a reprieve from the sentence already pronounced. Jesus has added the interceding 'vine-dresser'. Is this figure introduced because of a wish to make the description more vivid? Or is there a deeper meaning behind it? Does the figure of the gardener, pleading for the reprieve from the judgment, conceal Jesus himself? In this connection it should be remembered that the disciples must have understood the parables differently from the crowd or the opponents. As to the way in which the disciples understood it, the second alternative—cf. Luke 22.31f.—may very well be right.

But there is no going beyond the respite that God has granted. His patience is exhausted when the last day for repentance passes unheeded; and when that time has run out, no human power can prolong it (Luke 13.9). Then the door of the festal hall will be shut, and the word will be: 'Too late.' Two closely related parables describe what this 'too late' means; both deal with the closed door of the festal hall filled with guests. They are the *parable of the Ten Maidens* (Matt. 25.1–12; cf. Luke 13.25–27) and that of *the Great Supper* (Luke 14.15–24 par. Matt. 22.1–10).

Matt. 25.1f.: The parable of the Ten Maidens is one of those that begin with a dative (see pp. 79f.); the Kingdom of God is compared, not to the maidens, but to the wedding (see p. 80). 'Ten' is a round number, as is 'five' in v. 2. 'Who took their lamps and went': This is customarily regarded as the beginning of the story; the maidens start going with burning lamps, and the rest of the parable tells what happened to them after this, i.e. on their way. To this view, there are several objections. First of all, it is hard to picture a group of oriental girls sleeping (v. 5) in the open, especially in urban conditions (as are presupposed by the mention of 'dealers' in v. 9). Second, the place where they wait and sleep is not told; one would expect an indication of some sort if we were to imagine that this occurred somewhere along the girls' route. Third, the 'lamps' are not household lamps (Mark 4.21, etc.), usually made of clay, rather tiny and inapt for outdoor purposes, or lanterns (John 18.3), but torches (sticks with one end wound round with rags or tow soaked in oil).

They cannot have been burning while the girls slept. All these objections are met when we recognize that the relative clause at the end of v. 1 is not the first act of the happenings, but is part of the introduction of the parable which is in lieu of a superscription, just as the relative clause at the end of Matt. 22.2 is part of the superscription to the parable of the Great Supper. Thus the meaning of v. 1 is, 'That is how it is with the coming of God's Kingdom, as when a group of girls with torches brings in the bridegroom.' What the situation at the beginning of the parable is, is to be gathered from our next comment. 'To meet the bridegroom': The climax and the conclusion of the wedding celebrations came when the bridegroom fetched the bride from her home, and the bridal pair entered his parents' house. The bringing in of the bridegroom, with torches and other illuminations, is still customary in modern Palestine. Accounts from different parts of the country give us a complex picture, with details varying from village to village; but the one thing common to nearly all of them is that the climax and conclusion of the wedding celebrations is the bridegroom's entry at night into his parents' house. My late father described as follows a Jerusalem wedding that he attended in 1906: In the late evening the guests were entertained in the bride's home. After they had waited for hours, the bridegroom (whose arrival had repeatedly been announced by messengers) finally appeared, half an hour before midnight, to fetch the bride. He was conducted by his friends in a sea of lights from burning candles, and was received by the guests, who went out to meet him. Then, in a stately procession, the wedding party, again in a flood of light, went to the home of the bridegroom's father, where the marriage ceremony was performed and more refreshment was provided. As regards our parable, we have to picture the ten maidens in the bride's home, all set to go out but waiting for a sign of the bridegroom's arrival.

Verse 3: 'They took no oil with them': they neglected to bring flasks (see v. 4) with reserve oil which was needed because the torches would burn little more than a quarter of an hour. Verse 4: 'Flasks': small jars with a narrow neck. Verse 5: 'As the bridegroom was delayed': In modern accounts of Arab weddings in Palestine, we still hear quite often that people wait for hours for the bridegroom's arrival. The usual cause of the delay nowadays is the failure to agree on the presents that are due to the bride's nearest relatives; in antiquity it used to be a matter of haggling about the marriage contract in which the amount of money was specified that was to be paid to the wife if the union were ended through divorce or through the husband's death. To pass over this sometimes fierce haggling would be explained by the relatives' malicious indifference towards the bride; on the other hand it indicates flattery of the bridegroom if his future relatives show in this way that they are giving up the bride with the greatest reluctance. Verse 7: '[They] trimmed their lamps': they grab their torches, possibly pour oil on them, and light them. Verse 10: 'To the marriage feast': to the house where the wedding is to be; there they dance till the torchlight fails. Verse 12: 'I do not know you' is the formula of censure by which the teacher declines to have anything to do with a pupil for seven days; and so it means 'I will have nothing to do with you.'

This is one of the crisis-parables (see pp. 40f.). The wedding-day has come, the banquet is ready: 'The Lord our God the Almighty reigns. Let us rejoice and exult and give him the glory, for the marriage of the Lamb has come . . . Blessed are those who are invited to the marriage supper . . .' (Rev. 19.6, 7, 9). Only he who pays attention to the note of joy on which the parable starts (v. 1) can grasp the stern warning that it conveys: all the more let it be your concern to prepare yourself for the hour of trial and judgment that will precede the fulfilment. The hour comes as suddenly as the bridegroom in the night. Alas for those who are like those maidens who were foolish enough not to take reserve oil with them and who then found the door of the wedding-house shut against them. For them it is too late. For, as the *parable of the Closed Door* (Luke 13.24–30) adds, a parallel to the conclusion of Matt. 25.1–12, their appeal to the fact that they have enjoyed companionship with Jesus avails them nothing if their deeds have been evil (Luke 13.27).

'It may be too late' is also the message of the *parable of the Great Supper* (Matt. 22.1–10; Luke 14.15–24). In the Gospel of Thomas (64) it reads: 'Jesus said: A man had

guests, and when he had prepared the meal, he sent his
servant that he might invite the guests. He [the servant]
went to the first and told him: "My lord invites you." He
said, "I have money [to collect] from merchants. They are
coming to see me tonight, and I shall go and give them
instructions. I beg to be excused from the meal." He went to
another, and told him: "My lord has invited you." He said
to him: "I have bought a house, and it needs a day's
attention. I shall have no time." He came to another, and
told him: "My lord invites you." He said to him: "My
friend will be getting married, and I shall be in charge of
the feast. I shall not be able to come; I beg to be excused
from the meal." He went to another, and told him: "My
lord invites you." He said to him: "I have bought a village,
and am going out to collect the rent. I shall not be able to
come; I beg to be excused." The servant returned and told
his master: "Those whom you invited to dinner have made
excuses." The master told his servant: "Go out into the
streets, and bring in whom you find, that they may share
in my banquet." The buyers and merchants will not enter
my father's places.'

We have already seen that the parable of the Great Supper has
been so drastically edited by Matthew that it has been transformed into nothing less than an allegory of the plan of salvation.[1] On the other hand, in Luke and the Gospel of Thomas
(apart from a few expansions such as Luke's[2] doubling of the
invitation to the uninvited, and the expansion of the excuses in the
Gospel of Thomas[3]), the parable's original form has remained
essentially unchanged. Verse 16: The private person, who has
only one servant, is earlier than the 'king' (Matt. 22.2; see pp.
20, 55). The invited guests are well-to-do people, large land-
owners (see on v. 19). Verse 17: The banquet 'is now ready'. To
repeat the invitation at the time of the banquet is a special
courtesy, practised by upper circles in Jerusalem. Verse 19: 'Yoke
of oxen': Among the Palestinian Arabs the *feddān* is the com-
monest unit of land measurement; this is usually taken to be the

[1] See pp. 50ff., 55ff.        [2] See pp. 51f.        [3] See pp. 138f.

amount of land that can be ploughed in a day by a yoke of oxen. Besides this there is the legal *feddān* which corresponds to a year's work of a yoke of oxen, averaging, for good land, from 9 to 9.45 hectares. In general, a farmer owns as much land as one or two yoke of oxen can plough; that means about 10–20 hectares. As the man in the parable had just bought five yoke of oxen, he owned at least 45 hectares, probably much more, and was therefore a large landowner. Verse 20: 'I have married a wife' describes a recently completed transaction—'I have just been married.' Only men were invited to a banquet, and the newly married man does not want to leave his young wife alone. Verse 21: 'Maimed and blind and lame' people are *ipso facto* beggars in the East; they are invited, not out of compassion or from a religious motive (as in v. 13), but out of vexation. Verse 23: In addition to the beggars, the servant is to fetch the homeless from 'the highways and hedges' (see p. 51). 'Compel people to come in': even the poorest, with oriental courtesy, modestly resist the invitation to the entertainment till they are taken by the hand and gently pulled into the house. 'May be filled': It is of the utmost importance to the host that even the last place shall be filled. Verse 24: Who is meant by the 'I' ('I tell you', 'my banquet') is a disputed question. The plural 'you' does not agree with what has previously been said by the host, who in v. 23 addresses only one servant. It therefore seems, as in 11.8; 15.7, 10; 16.9; 18.8, 14; 19.26, to be the introduction to Jesus' final judgment; in that case 'my banquet' would refer to the messianic banquet (cf. Luke 22.30). Luke may well have understood it that way, and so have seen in the parable an allegory of the messianic banquet. In the Gospel of Thomas 64, too, the final sentence is understood as Jesus' words and connected with the heavenly banquet: 'Buyers and merchants will not enter my Father's places.' Originally, however, v. 24 will have been spoken by the householder, because (1) 'for' refers back to the command in v. 23, and (2) 'my banquet' corresponds to 'my house' in v. 23. But even if v. 24 is taken as spoken by the host, it breaks through the pattern of the story; it is a real threat only if it refers to the messianic banquet.

If this story were not so familiar, its unreality would strike us more forcibly. There are two features in particular that would seem absurd in real life: (1) the invited guests, one and all, as if by agreement, 'all alike' decline the invitation, and (2) in their place the host deliberately invites the beggars and the homeless. The conclusion that the whole thing is an allegory seems unavoidable; but such a conclusion would be wrong. On the contrary, Jesus was here using some well-known story material, namely the story of the rich tax-collector Bar Ma'jan and a poor scholar, which appears in Aramaic in the Palestinian Talmud. That Jesus knew this story is confirmed by the fact that he used it again: he used its ending, as we shall see later, in the parable of the Rich Man and Lazarus (see p. 145). We are told that the rich tax-collector Ma'jan died and was given a splendid funeral; work stopped throughout the city, since the whole population wished to escort him to his last resting-place. At the same time a poor scholar died, and no one took any notice of his burial. How could God be so unjust as to allow this? The answer is that although Bar Mc'jan had by no means lived a pious life, he had once done a single good deed, and had been surprised by death in the act. As the moment of his death had ensured that his good deed could not be cancelled by any further evil deeds, it had to be rewarded by God; and this was done through his splendid funeral. What, then, was this man's good deed? He had arranged a banquet for the city councillors, but they did not come. So he gave orders that the poor should come and eat it, so that the food should not be wasted.[1] In the light of this story we can now understand the strange behaviour of the invited guests in Luke 14.18–20. The host is to be understood as a tax-collector who has become wealthy and has sent out invitations in the hope that this will enable him to be fully accepted in the highest circles. But they all, as if by agreement, give him the cold shoulder, and decline his invitation on the flimsiest excuses. Then in his annoyance he invites the beggars to his house, to show the city magnates that he wants no favours from them and will have nothing more to do with them. Just as Jesus does not hesitate to illustrate from the behaviour of the deceitful steward the need for decisive action (pp. 36, 144f.), or from the conduct of the unscrupulous judge (pp. 123f.) and the assiduous search of the poor woman (pp. 106f.) the boundless mercy of God, so he does not in the least hesitate here to choose the behaviour of a tax-collector to illustrate both the wrath and the mercy of God. That the man's motive was just as selfish and ignoble as that of the judge who yielded to the importunate plaintiff simply in order to be left in

[1] The story is continued on p. 145.

peace (p. 123) did not disturb Jesus in any way, but rather induced him to choose just those persons as examples. The unprecedented seriousness of the conclusion (v. 24) is thus brought out. We must picture to ourselves how Jesus' hearers would smile at the description of the insolence with which the parvenu was treated, and of his consequent rage; we must imagine them breaking into hearty laughter at the thought of the upper ten scornfully watching from their windows the curious stream of seedy guests moving towards the gaily bedecked custom-house. How shocked they must have been when Jesus, the master of the house, sharply declared, 'The house is full, the number is complete, the last place is occupied; shut the doors; no one else is to be admitted.'

This parable, too, is not fully understood unless attention is paid to the note of joy that rings through the summons: 'All is now ready' (v. 17). 'Behold, now is the acceptable time; behold, now is the day of salvation' (II Cor. 6.2). God fulfils his promises, and is no longer hidden. But if 'the sons of the kingdom' (Matt. 8.12), the theologians and the pious circles, ignore God's call, the despised and the irreligious will take their place (see p. 51 above); the others will receive nothing but a 'Too late' from behind the closed doors of the banquet-hall.


## 6 The Challenge of the Hour

'It may be too late': the threat implied in these words tells what the hour demands; it calls for resolute action. That is the message of the *parable of the Debtor* (Matt. 5.25f.; Luke 12.58; see pp. 32f.).

Matt. 5.25: 'Your accuser', who has gone to court to recover a debt or loan. We must not use the expression 'lest some day' (Luther), implying that the action may take place some time in the future; the sense is rather 'lest [*sc.* before you know what is happening]'. 'And you be put in prison': Imprisonment for debt, and imprisonment as punishment in general, are unknown to

Jewish law. We must therefore infer that Jesus is referring to non-Jewish legal practice, which his audience considered inhuman, so as to impress on them strongly the terrible nature of the judgment. Verse 26: 'The last penny': the quarter of an *as* (in Palestine = 1/100 denarius) was the smallest coin in the Roman currency. Not a penny will be remitted; the scrupulous accuracy of the accounting illustrates how inexorably the sentence will be carried out.

You, says Jesus, are in the position of the defendant who will very soon be standing before the judge; on his way to court and under threat of arrest at any moment, he meets his opponent. Carried away by the scene that he depicts, Jesus exclaims beseechingly: Clear the matter up while there is still time. Acknowledge your debts. Ask your opponent for indulgence and patience (cf. Matt. 18.26, 29). If you do not succeed in doing so, the consequences will be terrible.

This parable is closely connected with that of the *Unjust Steward* (Luke 16.1–8).

Verse 1: 'A rich man': probably Galilean conditions are presupposed, the rich man being presumably the owner of a large estate managed by a steward who lives on the spot. 'Charges were brought to him': the East knows nothing of book-keeping or audit. Verse 3: '[He] said to himself' = 'he reflected' (there is no Semitic word for 'think', 'reflect', 'consider'). 'Dig': he is not used to 'working in the field'. Verse 4: 'I have decided' = 'it occurs to me now.' Verses 5–7: he will cover the embezzlements (v. 1) by falsifying the documents. The debtors are either tenants who have to deliver a specified part- half, a third, a quarter—of the yield of their land in lieu of rent, or wholesale merchants who have given promissory notes for goods received. 'A hundred measures' (*baths* in the Greek text, about 800 gallons) of oil corresponds to the yield of 146 olive-trees,[1] and a debt of about 1,000 denarii; 'a hundred measures' (*cors* in Greek, about 120 quarters) is 550 cwt., and corresponds to the yield of about 100 acres, and a debt of about 2,500 denarii. Very heavy debts were

---

[1] The average yield of an olive-tree in Palestine amounts to 120 kilos of olives, or 25 litres of oil.

therefore involved. The remission (400 gallons of oil and 24 quarters of wheat) is about equal in the two cases, since oil is much dearer than wheat; its currency value would be about 500 denarii. In this parable Jesus adopts the oriental story-teller's preference for large numbers. Verses 6f.: The steward has the promissory notes in his own keeping. He lets the debtors make their own alterations, hoping that the fraud, being in the same handwriting, will pass unnoticed; or he lets them make out fresh notes. Verse 7: He deals in the same way with the other debtors (v. 5). Verse 8: Probably 'master' (AV 'lord') originally referred to Jesus; see p. 34 above.

The shock, much discussed from early times, that has always been caused by a parable that seems to present a criminal as a model,[1] ought to disappear when we consider the parable in its original form (vv. 1–8) and disregard the expansions (vv. 9–13).[2] As in the parable of the Burglar,[3] Jesus is probably dealing with an actual case that had been indignantly reported to him. He deliberately chose it as an example, as he could be sure that it would secure the re-doubled attention of any hearers who did not know of the incident. They would expect him to end the story with an expression of strong disapproval, but instead of that, to their complete surprise, he praises the swindler. Are you indignant? Apply the lesson to yourselves. You are in the same position as that steward who saw disaster, his life in ruins; but the crisis that threatens you—in fact, you are already involved in it—is incomparably more terrible. That man was 'prudent' (v. 8a): that is, he realized that the situation was critical. He did not let things drift; he acted at the last minute before the threatening disaster overtook him, fraudulently and unscrupulously, no doubt—Jesus does not excuse his action, but we are not concerned with that here—but boldly, resolutely, and prudently, and gave

[1] The various attempts to whitewash the unjust steward have all failed.
[2] On the expansion of the text, see pp. 34ff.
[3] See pp. 37f.

himself a fresh start. For you, too, the challenge of the hour demands prudence; everything is at stake!

In face of this challenge of the hour, evasion is impossible. That is the message of the *parable of the Rich Man and Lazarus* (Luke 16.19–31).

To understand the parable in detail and as a whole, we have to recognize that the first part derives from well-known folk-material concerned with the reversal of fortune in the after-life. This is the Egyptian folk-tale of the journey of Si-Osiris and his father Setme Chamoïs to the underworld; it ends with the words: 'He who has been good on earth will be blessed in the kingdom of the dead; and he who has been evil on earth will suffer in the kingdom of the dead.' Alexandrian Jews brought this story to Palestine, where it became very popular as the story of the poor scholar and the rich tax-collector Bar Ma'jan. That Jesus was familiar with the story is shown by his using it in the parable of the Great Supper (see p. 141). We have already told the beginning of the story—how the scholar's funeral was unattended, while the tax-collector was buried with great pomp. Now here is the end of it. One of the poor scholar's colleagues was allowed to see in a dream the fate of the two men in the next world: 'A few days later that scholar saw his colleague in gardens of paradisal beauty, watered by flowing streams. He also saw Bar Ma'jan the tax-collector standing on the bank of a stream and trying to reach the water, but unable to do so.'

Verse 19: The rich man, who had no need to work, feasted every day, arrayed in a costly mantle of purple wool, with underwear of fine Egyptian linen. The lack of emphasis on his guilt—although, as his fate shows, he is represented as an impious reveller—is because Jesus was drawing on material that was well known to his hearers. Verse 20: Lazarus is the only figure in the parables who is given a name; the name ('God helps') therefore has a special significance. He is a cripple, suffering from a skin-disease (v. 21b).As a beggar (cf. John 13.29) he has his pitch in the street, at the gate of the rich man's mansion, where he begs for a gift from the passers-by. Verse 21: 'He desired to be fed' (i.e. he would have liked to be fed, but he was not). 'With what fell from the rich man's table' rather means, according to the Aramaic, 'with what was thrown on the ground

by those who sat at the rich man's table.' We are not to think of
crumbs, but of pieces of bread which the guests dipped in the
dish, wiped their hands with, and then threw under the table.
Lazarus would gladly have satisfied his hunger with them. The
dogs are wild, roaming street-dogs, which the scantily clad
cripple cannot keep away from him. According to the ideas about
retribution that were current in contemporary Judaism, his
miserable condition indicates that he is a sinner who is being
punished by God; and therefore the audience cannot have expected what followed. Verse 22: 'Abraham's bosom' denotes the
place of honour at the banquet at the right hand (cf. John 13.23)
of Father Abraham; this honour, the highest that could be hoped
for, indicates that Lazarus occupies the highest place in the
assembly of the righteous. He experiences a complete reversal of
fortune: on earth he saw the rich man seated at table, now he
himself may sit at the festal board; on earth he was despised,
now he enjoys the highest honour. He discovers that God is
the God of the poorest and most destitute. 'The rich man also
died and was buried': This funeral was, as is shown by the folk-
material mentioned above, a magnificent affair.

Verses 23–31 are concerned, not with the final fate, but with
the fate immediately after death, as we can see from the fact that
the brothers are still living on the earth. Verse 24: The rich man
appeals to his kinship with Abraham, i.e. to his share (which is
vicarious, by right of descent) in Abraham's merits. His modest
request shows how terrible is his torture: even a single drop of
water on his tongue from the springs that flow through the abode
of the righteous would alleviate his suffering. His kinship with
Abraham was acknowledged ('Son'), but not as entitling him to
salvation.[1] According to v. 25, it might seem as if the doctrine
of requital that is expounded here applied only to external
matters (wealth on earth, torment in the next life; poverty on
earth, refreshment in the next life). But, quite apart from the
contradiction in the context (vv. 14f.), where has Jesus ever
suggested that wealth in itself merits hell, and that poverty in
itself is rewarded by paradise? What v. 25 really means is that
impiety and unkindness are punished, and that piety and humility
are rewarded; this is clearly shown by a comparison with the folk-
material that Jesus used. As the material was well known, Jesus

[1] Cf. Matt. 3.9 par.; John 8.37ff.

merely suggests, without elaborating—on the one hand by the name 'Lazarus' which means 'God helps' (see on v. 20), and on the other hand by the prayer in vv. 27f., in which the rich man reveals his impenitence. Verse 26: The 'gulf' expresses the irrevocability of God's judgment; thus Jesus knows no doctrine of purgatory. Verse 27: 'Send him' suggests an appearance of the dead Lazarus, perhaps in a dream or vision. Verse 28: 'Warn' = 'entreat' (*sc.* with reference to tribu#retion after death). Verse 31 brings the climax. So far it has only been a question of an appearance of the dead Lazarus; now the idea actually emerges of his bodily resurrection. But even so great a miracle, transcending all the daily evidences of God's power, would make no impression on people who will not hear Moses and the prophets, i.e. who will not obey them. The reference to 'Moses and the prophets' as the substance of revelation (vv. 29, 31) is pre-resurrection (this also holds good for Luke 13.28); the expression does not exclude obedience to the messianic revelation, but rather, as is shown by Luke 24.27, 44, includes it, for this, in fact, brings the revelation in the law and the prophets to its fulfilment (Matt. 5.17).

The parable is one of the four two-edged parables (see p. 28). The first point is concerned with the reversal of fortune in the life to come (vv. 19–23), the second (vv. 24–31) with the refusal of the rich man's request that Abraham should send Lazarus to him and to his five brothers. As the first part is drawn from well known folk-material, the emphasis lies on the fresh part that Jesus added—on the epilogue. Like all the two-edged parables, this one stresses the second point. That means that Jesus does not want to comment on a social problem, or intend to give teaching about life after death—he tells the parable to warn people like the rich man and his brothers of the impending fate. Lazarus is therefore only a secondary figure, introduced by way of contrast; the parable is about the six brothers, and it should not be called the parable of the Rich Man and Lazarus, but the parable of the Six Brothers. The surviving brothers, who have their counterpart in the men of the flood generation, living a careless life, heedless of the roar of the approaching flood (Matt. 24.37–39 par.), are men of this

world, like their dead brother. Like him they live in selfish
luxury, deaf to God's word, in the belief that death ends
all (v. 28). Jesus was scornfully told by these sceptical
worldlings that he had better give them a valid proof of
life after death, if they were to take his warning seriously.
Jesus would like to open their eyes, but to accede to their
demand would not be the right way to do it. There would
be no point in performing a miracle; even the greatest
miracle, a resurrection, would be no use.[1] He who will not
submit to the word of God will not be converted by a
miracle. '*We are saved by hearing*' (Bengel). The demand
for a sign is an evasion and an expression of impenitence.
'No sign shall be given [i.e. God will give no sign] to this
generation' (Mark 8.12).

What is to be done? Jesus replied in ever-new similes:
Be on the watch (Mark 13.35), let your loins be girded[2]
and your lamps burning (Luke 12.35); put on the wedding
garment (Matt. 22.11–13). The meaning of these and
similar sayings is best illustrated by the *parable of the
Guest without a Wedding-garment* (Matt. 22.11–13).[3]

Verse 11: At formal banquets it is a mark of special courtesy
that the host does not share in the meal; he leaves the guests by
themselves, and simply appears during the meal. The missing
'wedding-garment' is not to be understood as a special garment,
worn only on festive occasions, but as a newly washed garment
(cf. Rev. 22.14; 19.8); the dirty garment is an insult to the host.
Verse 12: For the mode of address 'Friend' see on Matt. 20.13
(p. 109). 'How did you get in here?' = 'by what right [not
'by what means'] did you enter here?' 'And he was speech-
less', and so we are not told why he was not suitably dressed. Did
he slip in uninvited and feel ashamed because he was detected?
Or was his unauthorized intrusion a deliberate insult to the host,
and his silence a gesture of defiance? The rabbinic parallel cited

---

[1] Cf. John 11.46ff.; the raising of Lazarus completes the hardening of
the Jews.
[2] Girding consisted in tucking the end of the long loose garment into
the girdle, so that the garment did not hinder the work or get dirty.
[3] On the context, see p. 52. above.

below suggests another answer: he was invited, but he was foolish; the summons to the wedding-feast came earlier than he had expected, and found him unprepared. Thus the parable is one of the numerous crisis-parables (see pp. 36–50). The summons may come at any moment. Woe to the unprepared!

What exactly did Jesus mean by the clean garment which was the necessary condition for admission to the wedding-feast? Here we must choose between the rabbinic answer and the Gospel's. The rabbinic answer will be found in the Talmud (b. Shab. 153a) as follows: A Palestinian theologian of the end of the first century AD, R. Eliezer, said: 'Repent a day before your death.' His pupils asked him: 'How can a man know the day of his death?' He answered them: 'As he may die tomorrow, it is all the more necessary for him to repent today, and so he will be found in a state of repentance all his life. Moreover, Solomon in his wisdom has said: "Let your garments be always white; let not oil be lacking on your head" ' (Eccles. 9.8). In explanation of this saying there follows a parable of Rabban Jochanan ben Zakkai (d.c. AD 80) about a king who issued invitations to a banquet, without specifying the time. The wise attired themselves, while the foolish went on with their work. Suddenly the summons came, and those who were not dressed in clean clothes were not admitted to the banquet. Here the implication is unmistakable: the festal garment is repentance. Put it on before it is too late, 'a day before your death'—today. The demand of the crisis is conversion.

But there is another interpretation of the metaphor of the wedding-garment, one that stems from the Old Testament; and it is clear from the general tenor of Jesus' teaching that he had this second interpretation in mind. We read in Isa. 61.10 (a chapter to which Jesus attached special importance: Matt. 5.3f.; 11.5 par. Luke 7.22, see pp. 89f.; Luke 4.18f., see pp. 91f.):

'For he has clothed me with the garments of salvation,
    he has covered me with the robe of righteousness,

> as a bridegroom decks himself with a garland,
> and as a bride adorns herself with her jewels.'

God clothes the redeemed with the wedding-garment of salvation. Again and again Revelation speaks of eschatological clothing as the white garment (3.4, 5, 18), the royal robe of fine linen (19.8), which God will give. In these passages the white robe, or the garment of life and glory, is the symbol of the righteousness given by God (cf. esp. Isa. 61.10); and to be clothed with this garment is a symbol of membership of the redeemed community. It may be remembered that Jesus spoke of the messianic age as a new garment (Mark 2.21 par.; see pp. 91f.), and that he compared forgiveness to the best robe with which the father clothed the prodigal son (Luke 15.22; see p. 102); so we cannot doubt that this comparison underlies Matt. 22.11-13. God offers you the clean garment of forgiveness and imputed righteousness. Put it on, a day before the flood arrives, a day before the scrutiny of the wedding-guests— today!

Jesus thought of conversion as the wedding-garment and the shining light (Matt. 5.16), the face anointed with oil (6.17); it is music and dancing (Luke 15.25), because it means joy—the joy of the child returning home, God's rejoicing over the one sinner who repents more than over the ninety-nine righteous persons. But the return home is genuine only when it involves a renewal of life.

The first step on the homeward journey is to *'become like children'* (Matt. 18.3). It is well known that there are differing views about the essential point of this phrase, and many interpretations have been offered. But in any case we can take it as certain that 'children' means 'very little children'; that is how the Gospel of Thomas 22 takes it: 'These little [children] who are being suckled are like those who enter the Kingdom.'

We must disregard such interpretations as spring from western ways of thinking and are unsupported by oriental, and especially by biblical, usage, as, for example, the child is ready to receive, the child is naturally humble, and so on. This leaves us with three possible interpretations. First, it is a well established usage in Jewish baptismal terminology to compare the Gentile convert, as soon as he is baptized, to a 'new-born child', because in baptism God has forgiven him his sins. Here the child—that is, the very young child—is a type of purity. On this comparison, Matt. 18.3 would mean: 'If you do not become clean [through God's forgiveness] like [new-born] children, you will not be able to enter the Kingdom of God.' More probable is a second interpretation, because Matthew puts it forward in the context. He explains 'turn and become like children' by 'humbles himself like this child' (18.4); and that takes place through the confession of guilt, through self-abasement before God; and so we find in 18.4: 'Whoever humbles himself [before God,] [so as to become] like this child . . .' In this interpretation the force of the comparison with the child lies in the child's littleness, and to become again like a child means to become little again—that is, before God. But a comparison of 18.3 with the Markan and Lukan parallels shows that the saying was originally transmitted in isolation; only in a later stage of the tradition was v.4 (perhaps an altered form of Matt. 23.12b) set in its present context. We must therefore attempt a third interpretation of 'become like children'. Jesus' use of the word *Abba* (Mark 14.36) in addressing God is unparalleled in the whole of Jewish literature. The explanation of this striking fact is that *Abba* (= dear father) was an everyday family word, which no one would have ventured to use in addressing God. Jesus had authority to do so; he spoke to his heavenly Father as trustfully as a child to its father. Here we probably have the key to Matt. 18.3— it is children who can say *Abba*. 'If you do not learn to say *Abba*, you cannot enter the Kingdom of God.' In favour of this interpretation of 'become like children' are its simplicity and the fact that it is rooted in the heart of the gospel.

This, then, is the beginning of conversion and the new life—learning to call God *Abba* with childlike confidence, knowing that one is safe in his protection, and conscious of his boundless love. But we must recognize that becoming again like a child involves (Matt. 18.4) the confession of guilt (cf. Luke 15.18), humiliation, self-abasement, and becoming little again before God.

In the same way, the *simile of the Servant's Reward* (Luke 17.7–10) is a demand for the renunciation of all pharisaic self-righteousness.


The farmer here does not work on a large scale; he can afford only one slave, who has to work on the fields as well as in the house. Jesus asks: '(v. 7) Can you imagine that any of you would say to his slave who comes in from ploughing or tending the cattle, "Be quick, and sit down to your supper"? (v. 8) Would he not be more likely to say, "Get my supper ready, tidy yourself [see p. 148 n. 2] and wait on me till I have finished my meal, afterwards you can have your own supper"? (v. 9) Is he likely to thank his slave when he has carried out his orders? (v. 10) So should you, when you have done all that God has commanded you [see p. 11 n. 2] think[1]: "We are just poor[2] slaves; we have only done our duty." ' We have done nothing to merit God's commendation, and all our good works give us no claim on him.


But conversion goes further; it is expressed in acts, renunciation of sins, refusal to serve two masters (Matt. 6.24; Luke 16.13; Gospel of Thomas 47a),[3] obedience to God's command (Luke 16.29–31), obedience to Jesus' word. Just as a porter places on his neck and shoulders the yoke at each end of which there is a chain or rope to take the load, so Jesus' disciples are to take their Master's yoke on their shoulders;[4] Jesus' burden is lighter than that which formerly lay on their shoulders (Matt. 11.28–30). Everything depends on action; that is the message of the *parable*

---

[1] 'Say' here = 'think'; cf. Matt. 9.3 par.; 14.26. The Semitic has no exact equivalent of our word 'think'.

[2] The AV translation 'unprofitable' does not quite give the right meaning, which is rather 'miserable'. The text does not say that the fulfilment of one's duty is worthless, or that the disciples are lazy, unreliable servants; the word used is an expression of modesty.

[3] It was not unusual that a slave should have to serve two masters (e.g. Acts 16.16, 19), especially when brothers left an estate undivided after their father's death.

[4] Taking up Jesus' yoke means actually becoming one of his followers.

*of the Two Houses* (Matt. 7.24–27; Luke 6.47–49). As the torrential autumn rains, accompanied by storms, test the foundation of the houses, so the deluge will set in overnight and put your lives to the test. The Sermon on the Mount ends with the last judgment! Who will survive it? The 'wise man', i.e. the man who has recognized the eschatological situation. The Scripture said that only the house built on the sure foundation-stone laid in Zion would abide the onset of the flood (Isa. 28.15); 'he who believes will not be in haste' (Isa. 28.16). Jesus' contemporaries taught that the man who knows and obeys the Torah cannot be moved. Jesus takes them back to the Scriptures, but he gives a new answer, drawn from his own profound consciousness of authority: 'Every one who hears these words of mine and does them . . .' Merely knowing about his words leads to perdition; everything depends on obedience.

The obedience must be complete. The door of the festal hall where the banquet of salvation is to be held is narrow, and he who wishes to be admitted must strive for it while there is still time; many will seek to enter but will not make the necessary effort (Luke 13.23f.). It is particularly hard for the rich, the brutal rich of the East, of whom Jesus is thinking when he says that it is easier for a camel (the largest animal known in Palestine[1]) to go through the eye of a needle than for a rich man to enter the Kingdom of God (Mark 10.25 par.).[2] For Jesus assumes that his followers will be ready to make a complete surrender. The eschatological crisis demands a complete break with the past, and even, if necessary, with one's nearest relatives

---

[1] Cf. Matt. 23.24, where in the contrasted pair, camel and gnat, a contrast is drawn between the largest and smallest creatures of the Palestinian regions.

[2] The poorly supported reading *kamilos*, 'ship's cable' (instead of *kamēlos*, 'camel'), would be appropriate to the simile of the needle's eye; this has again been brought forward, though with flimsy backing, by G. M. Lamsa, *The Four Gospels according to the Eastern Version*, 1933. Against this very weak evidence is the rabbinic saying: 'You clearly come from Pumbeditha, where an elephant [the largest animal known in Mesopotamia] can go through the eye of a needle.'

(Luke 14.26 par.). That is what is meant by the metaphors of the dead left to bury their own dead (Matt. 8.21f.; Luke 9.59f.) and of *the ploughman who must only look straight ahead.*

The very light Palestinian plough is guided with one hand. This one hand, generally the left, must at the same time keep the plough upright, regulate its depth by pressure, and lift it over the rocks and stones in its path. The ploughman uses the other hand to drive the unruly oxen[1] with a goad about two yards long, fitted with an iron spoke.[2] At the same time he must continually look between the oxen to keep the furrow in sight. This primitive kind of ploughing needs dexterity and concentrated attention. If the ploughman looks round, the new furrow becomes crooked. Thus, whoever wishes to follow Jesus must be resolved to break every link with the past, and fix his gaze only on the coming Kingdom of God.

Jesus repeatedly deters the enthusiast by reminding him of the difficulties of discipleship; this is the object of the saying in Matt. 10.37f. par. Luke 14.26f., of the simile illustrating the homelessness of the Son of man (Matt. 8.19f.; Luke 9.57f.; Gospel of Thomas 86, here without introduction), and of *the saying about fire*, preserved in the Gospel of Thomas (82):

> 'He who is near to me
> is near the fire;
> He who is far from me
> is far from the Kingdom.'

These words are meant to deter: to be near Jesus is dangerous. It offers no prospect of earthly fortune, but involves the fire of tribulation and the test of suffering. But it must at the same time be borne in on everyone who, in allowing himself to be frightened away, rejects Jesus'

[1] Oxen were generally used for ploughing; cf. Luke 14.19, and on this see pp. 139f. above.
[2] Acts 26.14.

call, that he is excluding himself from the Kingdom of God. Indeed, fire is only a way through to glory.[1]

In the same way as these deterrent sayings, the *parable of the 'Tower'-builder and the King who would make War* is a call to self-testing (Luke 14.28–32). By the lesser example of the farmer whose unfinished farm buildings cause him to be ridiculed, and the more important case of the king who, in planning a campaign, underestimated the strength of his enemy and must therefore submit to his terms, Jesus drives home the exhortation: Consider it carefully, for a thing half done is worse than a thing never begun.

The *parable of the Return of the Unclean Spirit* (Matt. 12.43–45b; Luke 11.24–26) contains the same warning.

Both its language and its content are unmistakably Palestinian. Verse 43: An 'unclean spirit' is a Jewish synonym for a demon. In the desert, the natural abode of demons, he finds no rest, since he can be satisfied only where he can wreak destruction. Verse 44: The comparison of a possessed person to the 'house' of a demon is still common in the East. The house is 'empty, swept, and put in order', i.e. prepared for the ceremonious reception of a guest. Verse 45: 'He brings with him seven other spirits': his victim is an easy prey! Seven is the number of completion; the seven evil spirits represent every possible form of demonic seduction and wickedness.

The parable presents one great difficulty: it seems to depict the relapse, without reservation, as a universal fact of experience. But in that case Jesus' expulsion of demons would have been meaningless! The difficulty disappears if we realize that v. 44b has a conditional meaning: if he (the demon) on his return 'finds the house empty, swept, and put in order, then he goes and brings with him seven other spirits more evil than himself, and they enter and dwell there; and the last state of that man becomes worse than the first' (Matt. 12.44b–45a). The relapse is therefore not

[1] J. Jeremias, *Unknown Sayings of Jesus*, second English edition, London, 1964, pp. 66–73.

something predetermined and inevitable, but the man's own fault. The house must not remain empty when the spirit hostile to God has been driven out. A new master must reign there, the word of Jesus must be its rule of life, and the joy of the Kingdom of God must pervade it. It must be 'a dwelling place of God in the Spirit' (Eph. 2.22).

## 7 Realized Discipleship

This part of our subject must be introduced by the two *parables of the Treasure in the Field* (Matt. 13.44; Gospel of Thomas 109) and *the Pearl* (Matt. 13.45f.; Gospel of Thomas 76). They are closely connected, but will have been spoken on different occasions (see pp. 71f. above).

The completely distorted version of the first of these parables in the Gospel of Thomas is given on p. 23. Verse 44: A parable with a datival introduction (see pp. 79f. above): 'this is the case with the Kingdom of God.' 'Treasure hidden': Jesus will have thought of a jar containing silver coins or jewels. The numerous wars that swept over Palestine, as a result of her position between Mesopotamia and Egypt, repeatedly caused the burial of valuables in view of the serious danger. Hidden treasure is a favourite theme in oriental folklore; one is reminded of the Qumran Copper Scroll's account of fantastic treasures that are hidden away. 'Which a man found': The man is evidently a poor day-labourer; his ox sinks into a hole while ploughing. 'And covered up': He hid it again secretly. His aim is threefold: the treasure remains as part of the field, its safety is at the same time assured (burying was considered the best protection from thieves), and the secret is kept. The legal position is not considered; the procedure related would be that of the average person. At the same time it is worth noting that the finder does not just appropriate the treasure (about whose owner we hear nothing), but acts in a formally legal way by first buying the field.

In the Gospel of Thomas 76 the parable of the Pearl runs as follows: 'Jesus said: "The Kingdom of the Father is like a merchant who possessed merchandise and found a pearl. That merchant was prudent. He sold the merchandise, he bought the one pearl for himself." ' Matt. 13.45: Again a parable with a datival introduction (see pp. 79f. above). 'A [wholesale] merchant in search of fine pearls': The Gospel of Thomas has instead 'who possessed merchandise'; what he deals in is therefore an open question. If Matthew makes him a dealer in pearls, that is surely a secondary feature, since it anticipates the element of surprise. Pearls were highly valued during the whole of ancient times. They were fished up by divers, especially in the Red Sea, the Persian Gulf, and the Indian Ocean, and were used for adornment, especially as necklaces. We hear of pearls worth millions. Caesar presented the mother of his subsequent murderer Brutus with a pearl worth six million sesterces (£100,000); Cleopatra is said to have owned a pearl worth 100 million sesterces (more than £1½ million). Verse 46: 'On finding one pearl of great value': the stress is not on the 'one' (as if there were one pearl worth more than all the others), but on the adjective 'great'.[1] 'Sold all that he had': Again the Gospel of Thomas has the original, 'he sold the merchandise'. That is the only correct interpretation of the matter. Matthew has heightened the meaning under the influence of v. 44. There is no essential difference between the method of discovery in each case (in v. 44 the labourer comes on the treasure in the field unexpectedly, whereas in v. 45 the pearl is found after a long and laborious search), as the merchant was not an expert in pearls. In both cases the discovery is a surprise.

Both parables make use of favourite introductory themes of oriental story-telling. The hearer expects the story of the treasure in the field to be about a splendid palace that the finder built, or about a train of slaves whom he promenades through the bazaar (see p. 23), or about the decision of a wise judge that the finder's son should marry the daughter of the owner of the field, and so on. In the story about the pearl, he expects to hear that its discovery was the reward of special piety, or that it would save the life of a merchant who had fallen into the hands of robbers. Jesus, as always, surprises his hearers by treating well-known stories (pp. 140f., 145, 149) in such a way as to emphasize an aspect that they do not in the least expect. What aspect?

[1] For the linguistic basis of this statement, see the complete edition, *The Parables of Jesus*, London and New York, 1963, p. 200.

These two parables are generally understood as expressing Jesus' demand for complete self-surrender. It is really quite misunderstood if it is regarded as an imperious call to heroic action. The key-words are rather 'in his joy' (v. 44; they are not expressly repeated in the case of the merchant, but they apply to him as well). When that great joy, beyond all measure, seizes a man, it carries him away, penetrates his inmost being, subjugates his mind. All else seems valueless compared with that surpassing worth; no price is too high, and the unreserved surrender of what is most valuable becomes a matter of course. The decisive thing in the double parable is not what the two men give up, but the reason for their doing so: the overwhelming experience of the greatness of their discovery. So it is with the Kingdom of God. The effect of the joyful news is overpowering; it fills the heart with gladness, making life's whole aim the consummation of the divine community, and producing the most whole-hearted self-sacrifice.

What is the essential thing about the lives of people who have been overmastered by this great joy? It is that they follow Jesus. Its characteristic is the love whose pattern is to be found in the Lord who has become a servant (Luke 22.27; Mark 10.45; John 13.15f.). Such a love is expressed in silent giving with no sounding of a trumpet (Matt. 6.2); it does not lay up treasure on earth, but it entrusts its possessions to God's faithful hands.[1] It is a boundless love, such as is described in the *parable of the Good Samaritan* (Luke 10.30–37).

There are good grounds for contesting the usual view that the introductory verses 25–28 are simply a parallel to the question about the greatest commandment (Mark 12.28–34 par. Matt. 22.34–40). In fact, the only connection is the doubled command to love; all the rest is completely different, and it is quite likely that Jesus often expressed so central a thought as that contained in the double command. We have already seen (p. 89) that the

[1] Matt. 6.19–21; Luke 12.33f. It is not a matter of contrasting earthly with heavenly treasure, but of the place where the treasure is stored.

remark 'Great teachers constantly repeat themselves' (T. W. Manson) is true of Jesus. If we are right in supposing that the scribe, in repeating this command, was quoting one of Jesus' sayings, his 'desiring to justify himself' becomes intelligible; although he knows what Jesus thinks, he is justifying himself for asking him.

Verse 25: That a learned theologian should ask a layman about the way to eternal life was just as unusual then as it would be today; the probable explanation is that the man had been disturbed in his conscience by Jesus' preaching. Verse 28: When Jesus surprisingly tells him that action is the way to life, this must be understood as arising out of the actual situation: the inquirer's theological knowledge is no use unless his life is governed by love to God and to his 'companion'.[1] Verse 29: The counter-question as to what the Scripture meant by the term 'companion' was justifiable, because the answer was in dispute. It was generally agreed that it connoted fellow-countrymen, including full proselytes; but there was disagreement about the exceptions: the Pharisees were inclined to exclude non-Pharisees; the Essenes required that a man should hate 'all the sons of darkness'; a rabbinical saying ruled that heretics, informers, and renegades should be 'pushed down [into the ditch] and not pulled out'; and a widespread popular saying excepted personal enemies ('You have heard that God[2] has said: You shall love your fellow-countryman, but you need not love your enemy',[3] Matt. 5.43). Thus, Jesus was not being asked for a definition of the term 'companion', but for an indication of where, within the community, the limits of the duty of loving were to be drawn. How far does my responsibility extend? That is what the question means. Verse 30: The story with which he answers has, at least in its local setting, probably arisen out of an actual occurrence. 'He fell among robbers': The lonely descent from Jerusalem to Jericho, seventeen miles long, is still notorious for robberies. 'Who . . . beat him': The wounds (v. 34) suggest that the victim had defended himself.

Verse 33: According to the triadic scheme often employed in

---

[1] The import of the story is obscured if the translation 'neighbour' is used in Luke 10.29 already. The Christian conception of the 'neighbour' is not the starting-point of the story, but its upshot.

[2] The passive 'it was said' is a circumlocution for the divine name.

[3] Luke 6.27f. shows that this means a personal enemy.

stories, the audience would now have expected a third character, who would be (after the priest and the Levite) an Israelite layman; and the parable would therefore be expected to have an anti-clerical point. It would be completely unexpected to be told that the third character, who fulfilled the duty of love, was a Samaritan. The relations between the Jews and the Samaritans, which had undergone considerable fluctuations, had become much worse in Jesus' time, after the Samaritans, between AD 6 and 9, at midnight during a Passover, had defiled the temple court by strewing dead men's bones; and there was irreconcilable hostility on both sides. Hence it is clear that Jesus intentionally chose an extreme example; by comparing the failure of God's servants with the unselfishness of the hated Samaritan, his hearers were to measure the absolute and unlimited nature of the duty of love. Verse 34: He would hardly have a bandage with him, and he would probably use his head-cloth, or tear up his linen under-garment. 'Oil and wine': The oil would mollify (Isa. 1.6), the wine would disinfect (one would expect the reverse order). 'On his own beast': possibly the Samaritan was a merchant who carried his wares on an ass or mule, and rode a second beast himself. That he was a merchant who often went along that road is borne out by his acquaintance with the landlord and by his promise of an early return. Verse 35: 'Two denarii': the cost of a day's board would be about one-twelfth of a denarius.

Verse 36: A much discussed subject is the form that Jesus' question took—'Which of these three, do you think, proved neighbour to the man who fell among the robbers?' Whereas the scribe's question (v. 29) concerned the object of the love (Whom must I treat as a companion?), Jesus asks (v. 36) about the subject of the love (Who acted as a companion?). The scribe is thinking of himself when he asks: What is the limit of my responsibility? (v. 29). Jesus says to him: Think of the sufferer; put yourself in his place, and consider, Who needs help from me? (v. 36). Then you will see that love's demand knows no limit. But we must be on our guard here against over-interpretation. We can hardly say that the change in the form of the question conceals a deeper meaning. Both Jesus and the scribe are after the same thing: they are not looking for a definition, but for the scope of the idea 'companion', the only difference being that whereas the scribe looks at it theoretically, Jesus illuminates it with a practical example. Verse 37a: 'The one who showed mercy on him': he avoids using the hateful term Samaritan. Verse 37b repeats v. 28 with emphasis.

In this parable Jesus tells his questioner that, although 'companion' is certainly, in the first place, his fellow-countryman, the term includes more than that—everyone, in fact, who needs his help. The example of the despised half-caste is intended to teach him that no human being is to be beyond the range of his charity. The law of love calls him to be ready at any time to give his life for another's need (see p. 159 n. 1).

The boundless nature of love is also expressed in the fact that, following Jesus' example, it turns towards the very people who are poor and despised (Luke 14.12–14), helpless (Mark 9.37), and insignificant (Matt. 18.10). The value that Jesus sets on love to the needy and afflicted comes out in the description of the sentence pronounced at *the last judgment* (Matt. 25.31–46).

Verse 31: The messianic royal throne stands in Zion. Verse 32: 'Will be gathered' is a shepherd's technical term; the passive describes the divine action, which is here carried out by the angels (cf. Mark 13.27; Matt. 24.31). The gathering of the scattered flock is a feature of the messianic age (cf. John 10.16; 11.52). 'All the nations': That this passage describes the judgment of all the nations of the world is clearly shown by the word 'all'. 'Separate': This is also a shepherd's technical term. The Redeemer is the Shepherd (see p. 95), and he separates 'as a shepherd separates the sheep from the goats'. The Palestinian shepherd does not separate ewes from rams, but sheep from goats. In Palestine mixed flocks are usual; by day, sheep and goats are pastured together, but in the evening the shepherd separates the sheep from the goats. He takes the goats into the shelter of a cave, as they need to be kept warm at night, but he leaves the sheep in a penfold in the open, as they prefer the fresh air. Verse 33: 'At his right hand': the sheep are the more valuable animals; moreover their white colour (in contrast to the black of the goats) makes them a symbol of the righteous. The separation is the prelude to the final judgment. All that comes after v. 34

describes the promulgation of the sentence. Verse 34: The reference to 'the kingdom prepared for you from the foundation of the world' emphasizes the certainty of the promise. Verses 35f.: Six works of love, which are not meant to be exhaustive, are given as examples. With regard to the fifth of these works, the sick are poor, neglected people, for whom no one cares. The sixth (and last) work, the visitation of prisoners, does not appear in Jewish lists of good works. Verses 37–39, like 7.22, are a protest against the judgment that has been pronounced; the righteous do not know when they are supposed to have shown love to the king. Verse 40 gives them the explanation: it is not a question of the acts of love that they have shown to Jesus personally, but to his brethren, and through them to himself. The 'brethren' in this passage are not the disciples, but all afflicted and needy people. For the early Christianizing, especially in Matthew, of the word 'brother', see p. 84 n. 1. Verse 44, like 37–39, is an objection to the judgment. The unrighteous have never seen the king in distress, or heard him calling for their help. Verse 45: Their guilt does not lie in the commission of gross sins, but in the omission of good deeds (cf. Luke 16.19–31).

The commentaries on this parable refer to Egyptian and rabbinic parallels, which also talk of deeds of mercy as the decisive factor in the judgment. But what a difference! Both in the Egyptian Book of the Dead and in the Talmud the dead man boasts self-confidently of his good deeds ('I have given satisfaction to God by doing what he loves: I have given bread to the hungry, water to the thirsty, clothes to the naked' is what we read in the Egyptian Book of the Dead). How different is the surprised question of the righteous in vv. 37–39 of our passage, who are not conscious of having rendered any service, apart altogether from any idea that in the persons of the poor and wretched they had been confronted unawares with the hidden Messiah. This conception is attested as a characteristic of Jesus' preaching, and as belonging to the early tradition, by such sayings as we find in Mark 9.37, 41. Our pericope, although it may not be authentic in every detail, contains in fact 'features of such startling originality that it is difficult to credit them to anyone but the Master himself' (T. W. Manson).

Matt. 25.31–46 is concerned with a wholly concrete question, namely, by what criterion will the heathen (v. 32) be judged? Jesus had always clearly distinguished between present and eschatological justification. In the present time he mediates[1] God's forgiveness and release from the burden of guilt to returning sinners, to the lost and despairing, to 'God's beggars' (Matt. 5.3). On the other hand, he promises God's justification at the last judgment to the company of disciples when they should have been proved worthy by open confession of him (Matt. 10.32f. par.) and obedience (Matt. 7.21, 22f. par.), by readiness to forgive (Matt. 6.14f.) and merciful love (Matt. 5.7), and by endurance to the end (Mark 13.13 par.); at the last judgment God will look for faith that is lived. But even this justification of faith that is lived remains simply an act of God's free grace, and has nothing to do with merit; the guilt is too great for that. Perhaps, in view of such a saying as that in Matt. 10.32f., where Jesus says that he will intercede at the last judgment for those of his disciples who have confessed him before men, he might have been asked, But then, by what criterion will the heathen who have never known you be judged? Are they lost? (for such was the contemporary opinion). Jesus replies, in effect: The heathen have met me in my brethren, for the needy are my brethren; he who has shown love to them has shown it to me, the Saviour of the poor. So, at the last judgment, the heathen will be asked about the acts of love that they have shown to me in the form of the afflicted, and they will be granted the grace of a share in the kingdom, if they have fulfilled the Messiah's law (James 2.8), the commandment of love. Thus for them justification is available on the ground of love, since for them too the ransom has been paid (Mark 10.45).[2]

---

[1] Jesus mediates the forgiveness. In the same way as, e.g., in Mark 2.5, it is God who ultimately forgives. Jesus says (the passive being used as a circumlocution for the divine name): 'My son, God forgives your sins.'

[2] It is striking to observe how Paul's doctrine about justification corresponds with Jesus 'teaching, even in details. Paul also distinguishes between the justification of the sinner bestowed in baptism (I Cor. 6.11;

But the deepest secret of this love that is the mark of realized discipleship is that it can forgive. It passes on to others the divine forgiveness that it has experienced, a forgiveness that passes all understanding. The *parable of the Unmerciful Servant* (Matt. 18.23–35) is concerned with this.

On the context, see p. 7.7. Verse 23: We have here a parable with datival introduction ('It is the case with the [coming of the] Kingdom of God'; see pp. 79f.); the coming of the Kingdom of God is again compared to an accounting. 'With his servants': In the Bible and in the East 'the king's servants' is the term for his higher officials. Verse 24: One was brought to him who owed him ten thousand talents, i.e. 100 million denarii. The magnitude of the sum shows that the 'servant' is to be thought of as a satrap (governor) who was responsible for the revenue from his province (see below on v. 31); we know, for example, that in Ptolemaic Egypt the treasury officials were personally responsible for the whole revenue of their province. Even so, the sum far exceeds what the actual amount would be; ten thousand is the highest number used in reckoning, and the talent is the largest currency unit in the whole of the Near East. The size of a debt beyond all conception was intended to heighten the impression made on the audience by its contrast with the trifling debt of a hundred denarii (v. 28). The interpretation is therefore implicit in the parable: behind the king we see God, behind the debtor the man who was allowed to hear the message of forgiveness. 'Was brought': The passive indicates that the debtor is brought out of prison. Verse 25: First his lands and house property are to be sold. Jewish law allowed an Israelite to be sold only in case of theft, if the thief could not restore what he had stolen; the sale of a wife was absolutely forbidden under Jewish jurisdiction; thus the king and his 'servants' are represented as Gentiles. 'And children': A rabbinical parable describes how a king caused his debtor's sons and daughters to be sold, 'so it was clear that nothing more remained in his possession', i.e. the children are the last thing that a man can sell. Does the sale of

Rom. 6.7), by faith alone (Rom. 3.28), and the justification at the last judgment by faith working through love (Gal. 5.6). Paul also knows of a justification of the Gentiles at the last judgment, if they have fulfilled the unwritten law (Rom. 2.12–16).

the family make sense? As the average value of a slave was about 500 to 2000 denarii, the amount that would be realized from the sale of the family bore no relation to the gigantic debt of 100 million denarii, and so the king's order in v. 25 must be understood mainly as an expression of his anger. Verse 26: His servant's prostration, by which he indicates that he throws himself wholly on his lord's mercy, is the most urgent form of plea that there is. 'I will pay you everything': He promises to work out the debt. Verse 27: 'The king's mercy far exceeds his servant's plea (for a postponement of payment)' (M. Doerne).

Verse 28: In the street, he found one of his subordinate officials (see on v. 31). He seizes him by the throat; any attempted escape is made impossible. If he does not pay on the spot, he will be thrown into prison, or an order will be issued for his arrest (cf. Matt. 5.25f.). Verse 29: He is a minor official, for whom the payment of even a small sum will be difficult. His plea for postponement of payment corresponds word for word (except for 'everything' in v. 26) with that of the debtor himself; but there is this difference: the desperate promise in v. 26 cannot be fulfilled, whereas that in v. 29 can. Verse 30: 'In prison': the sale of the debtor (as in v. 25) does not arise here, as (according to Jewish law, which certainly held good elsewhere) it was allowed only when the debt exceeded the amount that would be obtained from the sale of the debtor, and this would not be the case where the debt was no more than a hundred denarii. In such a case, therefore, in Levantine countries, a writ of attachment was enforced, so that the debtor should work out the debt, or that his relatives should set him free by paying it. In Jewish law such a personal attachment of the debtor was unknown (see pp. 142f.).

Verse 31: 'His fellow servants': in the Greek translation of the Old Testament this expression occurs only in Ezra 4.7, 9, 17, 23; 5.3, 6; 6.6, 13, and it there denotes high officials, among them the governors of Palestine and Syria. This confirms the idea that the 'servants' are not common slaves. 'They were greatly distressed': 'they were shocked' (T. W. Manson). Verse 34: 'Jailers' (AV, 'tormentors' which is more literal): Punishment by torture was not allowed in Israel. It is again clear that non-Palestinian conditions are described here (see on vv. 25, 30), unless the parable refers to Herod the Great, who used torture freely, regardless of Jewish law—but could he have been credited with the generosity of v. 27? Torture was regularly used in the East against governors who were disloyal or who were tardy in their delivery of the taxes, in order to discover where they had hidden the money, or to extort the amount from their relatives or friends. The use, in legal proceedings, of non-Jewish practices that the Jews regarded as inhuman (see pp. 142f. on Matt. 5.25) is meant to stress particularly the frightfulness of the punishment. 'Till he should pay all his debt' can only meant that, in view of the magnitude of the debt, the punishment would be endless; once more (see on v. 24) the parable implies its interpretation. Verse 35: 'So also my heavenly Father will do to every one of you, if you do not forgive your brother[1] from your heart.' Forgiveness from the heart is here contrasted with forgiveness that is only with the lips (cf. Matt. 15.8 = Isa. 29.13). Everything depends on the genuineness of the forgiveness.

This is a parable about the last judgment; it combines an exhortation with a warning: God has granted to you in the gospel, through the offer of forgiveness, a merciful gift beyond conceiving. Ought you not to remit your brother's[2] trifling debt? God's gift puts you under an obligation. Woe to you if you try to stand on your rights, if you harden your heart and refuse to hand on to others the forgiveness that he offers to you. Everything is at stake, for God will then revoke the forgiveness of your sins and will see to it that his sentence is carried out in full. As elsewhere,[3] Jesus makes use of the Jewish doctrine of the two measures, but he completely transforms it. (It is no accident that there are no Jewish parallels to this parable.) Judaism taught that God rules the world by the two measures of mercy and judgment, but that at the last judgment he uses only the measure of judgment: 'And the most High shall appear upon the seat of judgment, and misery shall pass away, and the long suffering shall have an end: but judgment only shall remain . . .' (II [4] Esd. 7.33, 34a). Jesus, on the other hand, taught that the measure of mercy is in force at the last

---

[1] See p. 84 above.          [2] *Ibid.*
[3] Matt. 7.1f. par. Luke 6.37f.; Matt. 6.14f.; James 2.12f.; cf. Matt. 5.7; 25.31ff.

judgment too. The decisive question is: When does God at the last judgment use the measure of mercy, and when the measure of judgment? Jesus answers: Where God's forgiveness produces a genuine readiness to forgive, there his mercy grants forgiveness; but he who abuses God's gift faces the full severity of judgment, as if he had never received forgiveness (Matt. 6.14f.).

A second characteristic of discipleship is very strongly emphasized in Jesus' metaphors—the absolute safety of his disciples in God's hands. The simile of the slave and the son in John 8.35 assures them of their permanent right to the privileges of sonship in God's family, to which they now belong (Mark 3.31, 35; Gospel of Thomas 99). They are now not like underlings, but like the sons of a king (Matt. 17.24f.). They are clean like one who has bathed (John 13.10). Their utter security in the Father's care is depicted by Jesus in the incomparable images of the birds of heaven (Matt. 6.26; Luke 12.24) and the flowers of the field (Matt. 6.28–30; Luke 12.27f.). The full measure of the security of which these images speak can be estimated only by realizing their context. Jesus forbids us to 'be anxious'. The Greek verb *merimnān* that is used here can mean two things: (1) to give way to anxious thoughts; (2) to make exhausting efforts. That in Matt. 6.25–34 par. only the second meaning is intended can be inferred from Matt. 6.27 par. Luke 12.25, where the meaning 'to be anxious' does not make sense; and it is also shown in the two images, which refer, not to anxiety, but to effort. Thus, Jesus forbids his disciples to spend their efforts in trying to get food and clothing. Forbidden to work! How can that be? The words forbidding the disciples to work are, in fact, paralleled in Mark 6.8, where they form part of his charge as he sends them out on a mission. The field is vast, and time is short because the testing hour of the final crisis is at hand. The commission demands the utmost from the disciples, and so they must allow nothing to hinder them, not even an exchange of

greetings by the way (Luke 10.4b),[1] still less the expenditure
of effort for food and clothing. God will give them what
they need. What Jesus forbids to his disciples, therefore, is
not work but its duplication. But that, surely, may mean
that they have nothing to eat or wear, and must go cold and
hungry! Such anxieties are answered in the two similes of
the birds and the flowers, to which Jesus adds a touch of
humour. You men of little faith, he says, have you ever
seen Master Raven harnessing, ploughing, reaping, thresh-
ing, and gathering the harvest into barns? And yet God
amply supplies his needs. You men of little faith, did you
ever see Lady Anemone at the spinning-wheel or the loom?
And yet the royal splendour pales before the splendour of
her clothing. After all, you are God's children (Matt. 6.32;
Luke 12.30), and the Father knows what you need. He will
not let you starve.

These, he says, have a Father who cares for them, and
moreover they have a Master who calls them by name as
a shepherd calls his sheep (John 10.3),[2] and who prays
for them. The great crisis is imminent, to be ushered in
by Jesus' passion. The power of darkness is about to be
revealed in temptation of the most horrible kind, from
which there is only one way of escape—flee, so as to save
your soul (Mark 13.14ff.). Even Jesus' disciples will not be
spared. Satan, the accuser and destroyer of God's people,
has asked God's permission to sift them in the tempest of

[1] The oriental has plenty of time, and greatly dislikes hurrying.
Greetings involve him in long conversations. II Kings 4.29 gives instructions that are at variance with ordinary usage and politeness: 'If
you meet any one, do not salute him; and if any one salutes you, do
not reply'; it was a matter of extreme haste. In his prohibition, Jesus has
in mind the time-consuming business of joining a train of caravans for
protection against robbers.

[2] In modern Palestine, names are often given according to shape,
colour, and peculiarities (e.g. 'Grey-Ear', 'Short-Ear'); and the names
given to the lamb or kid are borne by the grown animal, as they are
familiar to it from their earliest days. The name is not only a device to
call the animal by, but also a sign of ownership. In leading his flock,
the Palestinian shepherd uses calls to make the animals come, go, or
stand still.

tribulation as a man separates chaff from wheat in a sieve (Luke 22.31f.).[1] And God has consented; it is his will. But Jesus has prayed for Peter, that his faith may hold fast, and that in the coming time of the final sifting he may again strengthen his brethren. Peter is the leader, and in praying for him, Jesus prays for them all. His intercession will bring them through, for Christ is stronger than Satan.

A third characteristic of discipleship is that God's gift and Jesus' call impel one to action. Just as Jesus likes to depict his saving mission under the figure of some special calling (see p. 95.), so he does with regard to his disciples' task. In the story of Peter's call in Mark 1.17, he describes the present fisherman as a future fisher of men. If a scribe becomes a disciple of the Kingdom of God, Jesus compares him to a householder who brings out of his store things old and new—the things that he had previously learnt, and his newly acquired knowledge (Matt. 13.52). The harvest is great, but the labourers are few (Matt. 9.37; Gospel of Thomas 73). The disciples are sent to the lost sheep of the House of Israel (Matt. 10.6)—presumably as shepherds, for so at least Matt. 18.12–14 understands it. As the steward appointed by Jesus himself, Peter holds the keys of the Kingdom of God (Matt. 16.19). In proclaiming the gospel, he and his fellow-disciples have authority to bind and to loose—that is, the authority to proclaim forgiveness, and where the message is rejected, to announce judgment; thus, as Jesus' messengers, they have judicial authority (Matt. 18.18; 16.19).[2]

The responsibility is immeasurable, and the time is short. Weal or woe, salvation or damnation, are at stake for innumerable souls (Matt. 10.12–15; Luke 10.5f., 10–12).

[1] Separation of chaff and wheat symbolizes the judgment (Matt. 3.12; cf. pp. 176f.).

[2] 'Binding and loosing' applies neither to scholars' authoritative decisions, nor to disciplinary measures, but to judicial authority to pronounce acquittal or condemnation. The best illustration is in Matt. 10.12–15, where Jesus' disciples bring peace and announce judgment.

The great and perilous task demands, as well as total devotion (see pp. 152–156), sincerity and God-given wisdom. Jesus expresses this in two similes closely related in content: 'Be wise as serpents and innocent as doves' (Matt. 10.16; Gospel of Thomas 39), and 'Have salt [= prudence] in yourselves, and be at peace with one another' (Mark 9.50b). Prudence includes spiritual sobriety, to which our Lord's much quoted but uncanonical saying[1] 'Be wise money-changers' is an exhortation. Just as the experienced money-changer recognizes a false coin at a glance, so Jesus' disciples are not to be misled by the false prophets who get the applause of the masses. Will they be equal to the task? In order that they may be, Jesus will not have them depressed, either in the face of opposition, or in view of their own lack of ability. The simile of the city set on a hill (Matt. 5.14b) reads in the Gospel of Thomas 32: 'Jesus said: "A city which is set on the summit of a high hill, and on a firm foundation, cannot be brought low, nor can it be hidden." ' This saying is meant to encourage Jesus' disciples, and to preserve them from despondency. They are, indeed, citizens of the lofty eschatological city of God (Isa. 2.2–4; Micah 4.1–3) which no earthquake, or hostile onslaught, or all the powers of hell (Matt. 16.18), can shake, and whose light shines out into the darkness, needing no human efforts. Having the gospel, they have all they need. If they have faith, even as little as a grain of mustard, the smallest of seeds, nothing will be impossible to them (Matt. 17.20; Luke 17.6).

Of one thing, however, they may be certain: they will not be spared the hate that Jesus encounters. Jesus has experienced the truth that a prophet has no honour in his own country (Mark 6.4; Matt. 13.57; Luke 4.24; John 4.44; Gospel of Thomas 31a), as the gospel is a cause of offence. The scholar can expect no better fate than his teacher, nor the slave than his master (Matt. 10.24f.; Luke 6.40; John

[1] J. Jeremias, *Unknown Sayings of Jesus*, second English edition, London, 1964, pp. 100–104.

15.20). Their mission involves the risk of life itself; Jesus sends them out defenceless, like sheep among wolves (Matt. 10.16; Luke 10.3). Some at least of the disciples must drain the cup of suffering together with Jesus[1] (Mark 10.38f.; cf. Mark 9.1.); for discipleship implies a readiness to lay down one's life, and to bear the cross (Mark 8.34 par.).

We generally think of one who, as the expression is, bears his cross, as one who patiently accepts whatever God sends; but there is no support here for this interpretation, nor does the phrase bear the meaning of readiness for martyrdom. It rather envisages a concrete situation, namely the moment when the man who has been condemned to cruxifixion, with the cross-piece laid on his shoulders, has to run the gauntlet of the howling, yelling crowd, as it greets him with insults and curses. The bitterness lies in the realization of being an unpitied outcast from the community, and exposed defenceless to abuse and contempt. Anyone who follows me, says Jesus, must expect a life as hard as the *via dolorosa* of one who is on the way to the place of execution. But even in death they are in the hands of one without whose will not even a sparrow[2] falls to the ground (Matt. 10.29; Luke 12.6). And they may learn from the example of the mother, how the bliss that awaits them will wipe out all memory of suffering (John 16.21f.). But however great their sacrifice and their success may be, the greatness of God's gift will keep them humble and guard them from pharisaic self-righteousness (Luke 17.7–10).

[1] To share the cup with someone means to share his fate, whether good or bad.

[2] A proverbially worthless creature. According to Matt. 10.29 two sparrows are worth one penny; according to the parallel in Luke 12.6 five sparrows are worth two pennies; if bought by the dozen, they are cheaper.

## 8 The Via Dolorosa and Exaltation of the Son of Man

Peter's confession marks the great division in the activity of Jesus. The public preaching is now followed by the message, revealed only to the disciples, concerning the suffering and triumph of the Son of man.[1] Already in his public ministry Jesus had used similes in speaking of his *via dolorosa*. He has no place to lay his head; he is homeless and must forgo even the shelter enjoyed by birds and foxes (Matt. 8.20; Luke 9.58; Gospel of Thomas 86)—a simile for his being rejected almost everywhere. From Caesarea onwards the imminence of the passion is fully disclosed to the disciples. In this case, too, Jesus often used metaphors. He spoke of the cup that he must drink (Mark 10.38; 14.36) and of the baptism that he must undergo (10.38). By dying he would create the redeemed community, for the shepherd must lay down his life for the sheep (John 10.11, 15);[2] he must be smitten with the sword (Mark 14.27 = Zech. 13.7), so that he may bring home the purified sheep (Mark 14.28);[3] the stone must be rejected (Mark 8.31; cf. 12.10 = Ps. 118.22), so that it may become the keystone of God's temple; the grain of wheat must die—and, we must add,

[1] Doubts have frequently been expressed lately on the historicity of Jesus' predictions of his passion. But although individual features were certainly formulated after the event, it can, in my opinion, be shown to be highly probable historically that Jesus expected a violent death, and that he found the necessity for his passion prefigured in Isa. 53. Cf. J. Jeremias, 'The Sacrificial Death' in *The Central Message of the New Testament*, London, 1965, pp. 31–50.

[2] K. E. Wilken, *Biblisches Erleben im Heiligen Land* II, Lahr-Dinglingen, 1954, p. 162, reports having heard from a shepherd of nocturnal attacks by more than thirty hyenas; he gave the names of friends killed in the fight.

[3] In Mark 14.28 the simile of the shepherd is continued, and the prediction in Zech. 13.8f. is taken up that after the shepherd's death the purified flock will reappear.

be raised again by God[1]—so that it may bring forth the full harvest of God's blessings (John 12.24; see p. 119). Such is the efficacy of Jesus' death, for it is the vicarious death of the sinless for the sinful, a ransom (Mark 10.45; Matt. 20.28) and a sacrifice (Mark 14.24) for the innumerable multitude of the lost.

But this passion of the Son of man, which represents the beginning of the final tribulation, is only the prelude to the last great victory of God (see p. 39). After three days Jesus will complete the new temple, whose foundation and erection (Matt. 16.18) were initiated through his earthly ministry, and of which he himself is the keystone (Mark 14.58 par.). As the lightning transforms the darkness into the clear light of day, so will be the arrival of the Son of man—sudden, unpredictable, and lighting up everything (Matt. 24.27 par. Luke 17.24).

# 9 *The Consummation*

When Jesus speaks of the consummation, he always uses symbols.

God is King, and will be worshipped in the new temple (Mark 14.58). At his right hand, on the throne, sits the Son of man (Mark 14.62), surrounded by the holy angels (Mark 8.38). Homage will be paid to him (Matt. 23.39). As the Good Shepherd he feeds the purified flock (Mark 14.28; Matt. 25.32f.).

Evil is banished: for the profaned temple has been destroyed (Mark 13.2), the sinful world has passed away (Matt. 19.28; Luke 17.26–30), the judgment of the dead and the living (Matt. 12.41f.) has taken place, and the final separation is completed (Matt. 13.30, 48). Satan has been thrown out of heaven (Luke 10.18), and, together with his angels, consigned to eternal fire (Matt. 25.41). Death reigns no

---

[1] As often happens in oriental usage, John 12.24, in the figure of the grain of wheat, mentions only the initial and final stages of the process when it says 'If it dies, it bears much fruit'. The important intermediate stage (the resurrection) must be supplied.

longer (Luke 20.36), suffering and sorrow have ceased (Matt. 11.5; Mark 2.19).

Conditions are reversed: what is hidden becomes manifest (Matt. 6.4, 6, 18; 10.26 par.), poor become rich (Luke 6.20), the last become first (Mark 10.31), the small become great (Matt. 18.4), the hungry are filled (Luke 6.21), the weary find rest (Matt. 11.28), the weeping laugh (Luke 6.21), mourners are comforted (Matt. 5.4), the sick are healed, the blind see, the lame walk, lepers are cleansed, the deaf hear (Matt. 11.5), prisoners are freed and the oppressed relieved (Luke 4.18), the lowly are exalted (Matt. 23.12; Luke 14.11; 18.14), the humble become rulers (Matt. 5.5), the members of the little flock become kings (Luke 12.32), and the dead live (Matt. 11.5).

Sinners are forgiven (Matt. 6.14), the Servant of the Lord has paid the ransom for the peoples (Mark 10.45 par.), the pure in heart see God (Matt. 5.8), the new name is bestowed (5.9), the heavenly angelic garb is conferred (Mark 12.25). They have eternal life (Mark 9.43), they live to God (Luke 20.38).

God recompenses (Luke 14.14): his great reward is paid (Matt. 5.12); in good measure, pressed down, shaken together, and overflowing,[1] it is poured into one's lap (Luke 6.38), the inheritance is distributed (Matt. 19.29), the treasure laid up in heaven is handed out (6.20), thrones and positions of authority are bestowed (19.28).

[1] Each of these four qualities has its own distinctive character. Even today the corn merchant tries to attract customers by crying out how completely his measure is filled. The measuring of the corn is a process that is carried out according to an established pattern. The seller crouches on the ground, with the measure between his legs. First of all he fills the measure three-quarters full, and shakes it well with a rotary movement to make the grains settle down. Then he fills the measure to the top and shakes it again. Next he presses the corn together very firmly with both hands. Finally he heaps it into a cone, tapping it carefully to press the grains together; from time to time he bores a hole in the cone and pours a few more grains into it, till there is literally no more room for a single grain. In this way the buyer is guaranteed an absolutely full measure; it can hold no more. That, says Jesus, is what God's measure will be like.

The glorified community stands before God's throne. Like Noah and Lot, it has been saved from the destruction (Luke 17.27, 29). The harvest is gathered into everlasting barns (Matt. 13.30), the new temple is built (Mark 14.58), the scattered elect are gathered together (Mark 13.27), God's children are at home in their Father's house (Matt. 5.9), the marriage is celebrated (Mark 2.19). After the tribulation, fullness of joy has begun (John 16.21). They live in eternal habitations (Luke 16.9), the Gentiles pour into the city on the hill, and feast with the patriarchs (Matt. 8.11) at the table of the Son of man (Luke 22.29f.). For them he breaks the bread of salvation (Matt. 6.11), hands them the cup with the wine of the new age (Mark 14.25), hunger and thirst are satisfied, and the joyful laughter of the messianic age resounds (Luke 6.21). The communion between God and man, broken by sin, is restored.

We do not know who the pious enthusiasts were who asked Jesus, presumably as a challenge, why he did not establish the pure messianic community by weeding out the sinners. It should never have been asserted that this question became a burning one only for the later community; the contrary is true. In Jesus' time there were attempts everywhere to set up the messianic community. First, we can think of the pharisaic movement. The Pharisees claimed to represent the holy community, the true people of God, as distinct from the mass of the people which, through ignorance of the law (John 7.49), was under God's curse. They were waiting for the Messiah, who, being himself 'pure from sin', would 'do away with sinners through his powerful word' (Ps. Sol. 17.36). There were also the Essenes (now known to us through their own evidence in the Qumran texts), who even surpassed the pharisaic attempt to establish the pure community, and tried to form the 'Community of the New Covenant', who emigrated from the city of the 'polluted sanctuary' (Damascus Document 4.18), and whose self-designation already indicates that they aspired to be the embodiment of God's people in the messianic age. Finally, reference must be made to John the Baptist, whose entire activity aimed at gathering the saved community, and who proclaimed that the Messiah would clear his threshing-floor and separate the chaff from the wheat (Matt. 3.12).

What Jesus did was the opposite of all these attempts. He aroused indignation by openly challenging the pharisaic community of the holy remnant, and by gathering round him the very people who were cursed because they 'do not know the law' (John 7.49). Among his followers were people who, not only by pharisaic standards, but also by his own, had no standing before God. Why did he allow this? Why did he not demand the separation of the pure community from Israel? The indignation aroused by Jesus' attitude was once more the occasion of parabolic teaching. His reply is contained in the *parables of the Tares among the Wheat* (Matt. 13.24–30) and of the *Seine-net* (13.47f.).

These two parables could hardly have been spoken as a pair (see pp. 71f.), but they are closely linked in content. The secondary (see pp. 66f.) representation of the setting (v. 36) should not lead us to regard the parable of the tares as addressed to the crowd (indicating that separation must await the end) and the parable of the seine-net as an exhortation to the disciples (Throw out the net, you fishers of men!). For this second interpretation is refuted by the datival introduction (see below on v. 47). The parable of the tares among the wheat is given in the Gospel of Thomas 57 as follows: 'Jesus said, "The Kingdom of the Father is like a man who had good seed. His enemy came by night and sowed a weed among the good seed. The man did not permit them [= his servants] to pull up the weed. He said to them: Lest perhaps you go to pull up the weed and pull up the wheat with it. For on the day of harvest the weeds will appear [or: come to light]. They will pull them and burn them." ' It will be seen that the ending in particular is shorter than in Matthew, who, anticipating his allegorical interpretation (see pp. 66f.) may have somewhat over-elaborated the separation of wheat from tares (v. 30). Verse 24: 'It is with the Kingdom of God as with a man . . .' The comparison is not with the man, but with the harvest (see p. 80). Verse 25: As a similar occurrence is reported from modern Palestine, Jesus may have had in mind an actual event. The weed is the poisonous bearded darnel, closely related botanically to the bearded wheat, and, in the early stages of growth, resembling it. Verse 26: The darnel shoots up in much more than normal quantities. Verse 28: 'An enemy has done this.' So far, then, the whole of the introductory vv. 24–28a is intended to make it clear that the owner is not to blame for the great quantity of weeds. The real problem is first stated in the servants' question (v. 28b), whether they are to uproot the weeds. This question is by no means a foolish one; it is usual to weed out darnel, even repeatedly. Verse 29: The master of the house is of the opinion that the darnel must be left alone, obviously because of its unusual quantity, which means that the roots have become intertwined with those of the wheat. Verse 30: 'The reapers': at harvest time reapers are employed besides the regular servants. 'Gather the weeds first': by the gathering of the darnel we are not to understand that it was rooted up immediately before the grain was reaped, but that, as the reaper cut the grain with his sickle, he let the darnel fall, so that it was not gathered into the sheaves. 'Bind them in bundles': the binding of the darnel into bundles is not an unnecessary piece of work; it was evidently to be dried and used for fuel; Palestine is lacking in forests, and so fuel is scarce (cf. Matt. 6.30).

To understand the parable of the seine-net (Matt. 13.47f.) it is essential to recognize that we have here another of the parables with a datival introduction; the Kingdom of God is therefore not compared to a net, which catches good and bad fish and preserves them; but the opening formula (v. 47) must be translated: 'It is the case with the coming of the Kingdom of God'—namely, as with the sorting of the fish (see p. 80). The net is a drag-net, which is either dragged between two boats or laid out by a single boat and pulled to the land with long ropes. 'Of every kind' merely explains the need for the selection described in v. 48; the net contained fish 'of every kind', edible and inedible (so there is no allegorical reference to the Gentile mission). In the Lake of Gennesaret twenty-four different kinds of fish have been counted. Verse 48: 'The bad' are (a) unclean fish (Lev. 11.10f.: all fish without scales and all without fins), and (b) non-edible aquatic creatures, such as crabs, which were regarded as worthless.

Both parables are eschatological in character, since both
are concerned with the final judgment which ushers in the
Kingdom of God; it is compared to a separation—in the
former parable between wheat and weeds, and in the latter
between edible and inedible fish. Before the separation, good
and bad are mixed. In the parable of the tares, the idea of a
premature separation is expressly rejected, and patience
until the harvest is enjoined. Why is such patience necessary?
Jesus gives two reasons. First, men are not capable of carrying out the separation properly (Matt. 13.29). As, in the
early stages of growth, darnel and wheat are confusingly
alike, so the hidden Messiah's people of God are concealed
among the false believers. Men cannot see into the heart;
if they tried to carry out the separation, they would in-
evitably make wrong judgments and uproot good wheat
with the weeds.[1] Instead, God has fixed the moment of
separation. The measure of time that he has laid down must
be fulfilled (Matt. 13.48), the seed must be allowed to ripen.
Then comes the end,[2] and with it the separation of tares and
wheat, the sorting of the fish with the dividing of the good
from the bad. Then, no longer in the form of a servant,
God's holy community, purged of all evil men, false
believers, and feigned confessors, will be revealed at last.
But that moment has not yet come; the last opportunity
for repentance has not yet run out (Luke 13.6–9). Till then,
all false zeal must be checked, the fields must be left to
ripen in patience, the net must be cast widely, and everything else left to God in faith, till his hour comes.[3]

[1] Cf. I Cor. 4.5: 'Do not pronounce judgment before the time.'
[2] See pp. 92f.
[3] This attitude of Jesus is firmly embedded in the tradition. He
repeatedly emphasizes the warning that the band of disciples is not a
purified community, and that at the end it must undergo separation
(Matt. 7.21–23, 24–27; 22.11–14). He also calls for patience (Mark
4.26–29; see pp. 120f.).

# 10 Parabolic Actions

This aspect of our subject can only be treated briefly here as a short supplement. Jesus did not confine himself to spoken parables, but also performed parabolic actions. His most significant parabolic action was to give hospitality to the outcasts (Luke 19.5f.) and to receive them into his house (Luke 15.1f.), and even into the circle of his disciples (Mark 2.14 par.; Matt. 10.3). These feasts for tax-collectors are prophetic signs, more impressive than words, and proclaiming unmistakably that the messianic age is here, and that it is the age of forgiveness.[1] On the night before his death he made use of the common meal to perform the last symbolic act of his life, by offering to his own a share in the atoning efficacy of the death that awaited him.

Jesus continually found new ways of proclaiming by his acts the advent of the messianic age: by the healings, by the rejection of fasting (Mark 2.19f. par.), by bestowing on Simon the son of Jona the new name of Peter, thus designating him as the foundation-stone of the eschatological temple of God, the building of which had now begun (Matt. 16.17f.). He expressed his sovereignty as Lord of the eschatological people of God (including the nine and a half lost tribes) in the symbolic number of his disciples, his royal authority by his kingly entry into Jerusalem and his cleansing of the temple (both of which acts are inseparably connected as a symbol of the coming new age), the peaceful purpose of his mission by the choice of an ass on which to make his entry (cf. Zech. 9.9). He rebuked his ambitious disciples by setting a child in their midst (Mark 9.36 par.); he washed their feet as an example of the love that stooped to serve (John 13.1ff.). If we may assume that the story of the adulteress ([John] 7.53ff.) rests on early tradition, then the writing in the sand (8.6, 8) is another example of parabolic

---

[1] J. Schniewind, *Das Evangelium nach Markus*, Das Neue Testament Deutsch 1¹⁰, Göttingen, 1963, on Mark 2.5.

action; it would remind her accusers, without openly shaming them, of the Scripture that said: 'Those who turn away from thee shall be written in the earth' (Jer. 17.13), and would say to them: 'You are those who turn away'[1]— a silent call to repentance.[2] Jesus' weeping over Jerusalem can also be included among the symbolic actions, as a prophetic anticipation of sorrow over its approaching fate. The great majority of his symbolic actions announce that the messianic age has dawned. Jesus, in fact, not only proclaimed the parables' message; he lived it and embodied it in his own person. 'Jesus not only utters the message of the Kingdom of God; he himself is the message'.[3]

[1] The writing of a name in the sand so that the wind may carry it away indicates proscription and a threat of destruction.

[2] Another interpretation of the writing in the sand is that Jesus was acting like a Roman judge who wrote down his sentence before reading it out. Jesus' sentence was—Acquittal.

[3] C. Maurer in *Judaica* 4 (1948), p. 147.

# IV

## CONCLUSION

IN OUR attempt to recover the original significance of
the parables, one thing above all becomes evident: all
Jesus' parables compel his hearers to define their attitude
towards his person and mission. For they are all full of
'the secret of the Kingdom of God' (Mark 4.11)—that is to
say, the certainty that the messianic age is dawning. The
hour of fulfilment has come; that is the keynote of them all.
The strong man is disarmed, the powers of evil have to
yield, the physician has come to the sick, the lepers are
cleat sed, the heavy burden of guilt is removed, the lost
sheep is brought home, the door of the Father's house is
opened, the poor and the beggars are summoned to the
banquet, a master whose kindness is undeserved pays wages
in full, a great joy fills all hearts. God's acceptable year has
come. For there has appeared the one whose veiled majesty
shines through every word and every parable—the Saviour.

# APPENDICES

# A. GLOSSARY

## by Dr Berndt Schaller

*Apocalyptic*. Relating to a line of thought that developed in Judaism after the OT prophets; this continued in primitive Christianity, and was determined by the supposedly imminent end of the world. The apocalyptists' ideas, which were recorded in numerous apocalypses, of which the best known is the Book of Enoch, revolve round the mysteries of the universe, of world history, and in particular of what will happen in the last days.

*Apocrypha*. Certain religious writings that were not received into the canon of the OT or NT. The NT apocrypha include (*a*) gospels (e.g. the Gospel of the Nazarenes, see p. 45 n. 1, and the Gospel of Thomas), and (*b*) apostolic acts and letters, mostly originating in heretical circles, and intended to supplement or replace the NT writings. A handy collection of what is left of the NT Apocrypha is M.R. James, *The Apocryphal New Testament*, Oxford, 1924 = 1953.

*Council* (*Sanhedrin*). The highest Jewish authority before AD 70 on religious, legal and administrative questions. Its seventy-one members (Sanhedrists) came from the priestly and secular aristocracy, as well as from the ranks of the scribes (Mark 11.27 par.; 14.53).

*Editing*. The final arrangement and revision, by the evangelists, of the component parts of the primitive Christian tradition (see *Form criticism*) relating to Jesus' life and preaching. It is to their work as editors that we owe the Gospels in their present form.

*Essenes*. A Jewish ascetic community, existing roughly from the second century BC to the first AD with a hierarchical organization (priests, Levites, laity). In their peculiarities and aims they were akin to the Pharisees, seeking to show themselves as the real people of God through strict observance of the OT law. They lived in closed groups, their centre being at Qumran on the Dead Sea. The discoveries made there since 1947 have brought to light many Essene writings, which give us a more detailed insight into the community's life and doctrines.

*Form criticism.* The Gospels, as we now have them, are the product of a complex development of the tradition (see *Editing*). This began as independent items consisting of bits of Jesus' words and deeds which were handed down orally in rather well defined forms (such as parables, beatitudes, miracle stories, controversy stories, etc.). These do not owe their characteristics to chance; on the contrary, they were moulded by definite sociological factors—those which constituted the concrete situation in the life of the Early Church in which the material was used (*Sitz im Leben*). Form criticism therefore often enables us to infer the original designation as well as the later practical application of the individual items, and so to outline a picture of their origin and their history within the tradition. Part II of the present work analyses the parables of Jesus in the light of form criticism.

*Gnosis.* A Greek word meaning 'knowledge', 'cognition'; from it comes 'gnosticism', a widespread complex religious movement in the first centuries of our era. Its essential characteristic was the desire for knowledge of God, the world, and the self, as the way to redemption.

*Midrash.* Rabbinic commentary on an OT book.

*Parousia.* A Greek word meaning 'presence', 'arrival'; in Christian language, the second coming of Christ.

*Pharisees.* A religious lay movement from the second century BC onwards. The members formed closed communities led by scribes. On being admitted into the community, they undertook to observe rigidly the regulations as to tithes and purification (cf. Matt. 23.23–26 par. Luke 11.39–42). They thereby claimed to represent God's people in its purity, and consequently kept apart from the common people (thus the name *Pharisees* = 'separated'). In contrast to the Sadducees, they respected and cultivated the oral traditions of law and doctrine. They maintained a political neutrality towards the Romans.

*Redaction.* See *Editing.*

*Sadducees.* Members of a strongly conservative party within the Jewish people before AD 70. They belonged mainly to the priestly and secular aristocracy, and were theologically opposed to the Pharisees. Thus they rejected all oral tradition, and maintained that only the written *Torah* was valid. In politics they were friendly towards the Romans.

*Septuagint.* Jewish Greek version of the OT (pre-Christian).

*Sitz im Leben.* See *Form criticism.*

*Soteriology.* The concept and doctrine of the redemption of man and the world.

*Synoptists.* The evangelists Mark, Matthew, and Luke, whose Gospels largely correspond in material and construction, and so may be printed in parallel columns in form of a synopsis (Greek, 'joint or general view') so as to be studied side by side.

*Talmud.* The most comprehensive collection of rabbinic learning. There are the *Jerusalem* (or *Palestinian*) *Talmud* (redaction concluded early in the fifth century AD), and the *Babylonian Talmud* (redaction concluded in the sixth century AD). They contain the discussion of the rabbinic schools of Palestine and Babylonia respectively on the Mishnah (a collection of religious ordinances, finally edited about AD 200).

*Torah.* A Hebrew word for 'instruction' or 'law'. In ancient Judaism it denotes, in the narrower sense, the Pentateuch, or first five books of the OT (cf. Matt. 5.17; Luke 2.23), and in the wider sense, the whole of the OT (cf. John 10.35).

*Zealots.* Followers of a movement, both religious and nationalist, within ancient Judaism, seeking to force the arrival of the messianic kingdom by political means. They originated the insurrections against Rome, whose rule they contested in order to set up the rule of God.

# B. INDEX OF SYNOPTIC PARABLES

*\* = literal quotation of the version of the Gospel of Thomas*

Mark 4.3–8; Matt. 13.3–8; Luke 8.5–8; Thomas 9:
*The Sower*                                9f., 20\*, 64; 119f.

Mark 4.26–29:
*The Patient Husbandman*                                120f.

Mark 4.30–32; Matt. 13.31f.; Luke 13.18f.; Thomas 20:
*The Mustard-seed*                                80, 116ff.\*

Mark 12.1–11; Matt. 21.33–44; Luke 20.9–18; Thomas 65:
*The Wicked Husbandmen*                     57ff\*., 100, 132

Mark 13.28f.; Matt. 24.32f.; Luke 21.29–31:
*The Budding Fig-tree*                                93f.

Mark 13.33–37; Luke 12.35–38:
*The Doorkeeper*                                41ff., 131

Matt. 5.25f.; Luke 12.58f.:
*Going before the Judge*                                32f., 142f.

Matt. 7.24–27; Luke 6.47–49:
*Two Houses*                                153

Matt. 11.16–19; Luke 7.31–35:
*The Children in the Market-place*                                127f.

Matt. 12.43–45; Luke 11.24–26:
*The Return of the Unclean Spirit*                                155f.

Matt. 13.24–30; Thomas 57:
*The Tares among the Wheat*                                66f., 176ff.\*

Matt. 13.33; Luke 13.20f.; Thomas 96:
*The Leaven*                                80, 116ff.\*

Matt. 13.44; Thomas 109:
*The Treasure*                                23f\*., 156ff.

Matt. 13.45f.; Thomas 76:
The Pearl     156ff.*

Matt. 13.47f.:
The Seine-net     80, 176ff.

Matt. 18.12–14; Luke 15.4–7; Thomas 107:
The Lost Sheep     29ff., 105ff.*

Matt. 18.23–35:
The Unmerciful Servant     164ff.

Matt. 20.1–16:
The Good Employer     24ff., 108ff.

Matt. 21.28–32:
The Two Sons     65f., 98, 100

Matt. 22.1–10; Luke 14.16–24; Thomas 64:
The Great Supper     33f*., 50ff., 55ff., 138ff*.

Matt. 22.11–14:
The Guest without a Wedding Garment     51ff. 148ff.

Matt. 24.43f.; Luke 12.39f.; Thomas 21b, 103:
The Burglar     37ff., 69*, 75*, 129

Matt. 24.45–51; Luke 12.42–46:
The Servant entrusted with Supervision     44ff., 81, 131

Matt. 25.1–13:
The Ten Maidens     39ff., 136ff.

Matt. 25.14–30; Luke 19.12–27:
The Talents     45ff., 131

Matt. 25.31–46:
The Last Judgment     161ff.

Luke 7.41–43:
The Two Debtors     98ff., 115

Luke 10.25–37:
The Good Samaritan     158ff.

Luke 11.5–8:
The Friend asked for Help at Night     124ff.

Luke 12.16–21; Thomas 63:
The Rich Fool     129f.*

Luke 13.6–9:
The Barren Fig-tree     129, 135f.

Luke 13.24–30:
*The Closed Door* 76

Luke 14.28–32:
*The Tower-builder and the King who would make War* 155

Luke 15.8–10:
*The Lost Coin* 105ff.

Luke 15.11–32:
*The Father's Love* (*The Prodigal Son*) 101ff.

Luke 16.1–8:
*The Unjust Steward* 34ff., 143ff.

Luke 16.19–31:
*The Rich Man and Lazarus* 145ff.

Luke 17.7–10:
*The Servant's Reward* 152

Luke 18.1–8:
*The Unjust Judge* 122ff.

Luke 18.9–14:
*The Pharisee and the Tax-collector* 111ff.